GUEST AFLOAT

11/16/16

Happy cruising,
Celia & Gordon
You never know... this
may come in handy

Barbara

GUEST AFLOAT

The essential guide
to being a welcome guest
on board a boat

Barbara Bradfield and Sara Slater

Marlor Press, Inc.
Saint Paul, Minnesota

GUEST
AFLOAT

A Marlin Bree Book
Published by Marlor Press, Inc.

Copyright 1997 by Barbara Bradfield and Sara Slater
Illustrated by Sara Slater and Barbara Bradfield
Chapter heading illustrations by Ellie Lander
Cover design by MacLean & Tuminelly

ISBN 0-943400-94-5
Manufactured in the United States of America
First Edition

Disclaimer: This book is intended only as a general guide to boating and boating practices. Readers should use their own judgement and discretion on specific facilities, practices and events. Not responsible for errors and ommissions. In any event, Marlor Press and the authors are not responsible for damages, loss or injury of any kind.

Library of Congress Cataloging-in-Publication Data

Bradfield, Barbara
  Guest afloat : the essential guide to being a welcome guest on board a boat / Barbara Bradfield and Sara Slater. -- 1st ed.
     p.   cm.
  "A Marlin Bree book" -- T.p. verso.
  Includes index.
  ISBN 0-943400-94-5
  1. Boat living. 2. Sailboat living. 3. Hospitality. 4. Etiquette. I. Slater, Sara (Sara Sanford) II. Title.
GV777.7.B73 1997   97-49924
797.1--dc21   CIP

MARLOR PRESS, INC.
4304 Brigadoon Drive
Saint Paul, Minnesota 55126

CONTENTS

To our husbands for sharing their boating world
and our children for happy memories,
great adventures

BEING A GUEST AFLOAT

When I was little, I loved the water so much that I wanted to be a boat. An older sister, who was my captain, convinced me to tie the corners of a sheet to my ankles and wrists, straddle the middle seat of our rowboat, turn my back to the wind — and brace myself.

Off we sailed, careening over the choppy depths somewhat perilously and certainly out of control. Though not quite a boat, I was thrilled beyond imagination to at least be a sail.

Boating these days, although safer and less primitive, still brings that unquenchable joy of being on the water. Life can't get much better than this: wake to the gulls busy with their morning action, the soft chatter of stones chuckling against the beach, the gently lapping waves against the hull, the shimmering reflections of light through the ports. There is motion underfoot, reminding you that your boat is in her natural element and, in her own way, alive.

Every day spent aboard reconfirms my old love of the water, where the air is clear, the stars are bright, the food tastes great and, when day ends, sleep is deep.

Guests make boating even better. Their enthusiasm and fresh vision, whether they're first-timers or old hands, is contagious. It invigorates and renews my own appreciation of life aboard and gives me a good excuse to perk up the menu, plan fun activities and sift through pleasant memories to map out a special cruise.

Guests stepping aboard may feel a bit unsettled until they come to know what to expect. After all, being on a boat for the first time is like entering a new world with a new nautical language. Where shall I go? What can I do with my stuff and not look stupid? Is there anything I shouldn't do or touch? Am I in the way? How do I help when I don't know what is needed? I'm hungry. Can I fix a snack? How far will the boat tip? Will the Captain yell at me if I ask too many questions? And what, exactly, is he or she telling me? This is pretty cool, but when will I have it all figured out so I can start singing chanteys?

Guests, tell yourself this: slow down, take a deep breath and relax. You have left behind freeways and commutes, shops and marketing, schools and meetings, the doorbell and telephone, mail to sort and paper to read...in short, your busy regular schedule. A boat is a place, above all else, apart. You have time to consciously tune in to a pleasant, slower pace. Life is simplified, space is limited, there are fewer people and distractions. Your big job now is to surrender to that seductive pull of life at sea.

Even well-intentioned people need to know more about being a good guest afloat. With an understanding of basic sea knowledge and boating etiquette, guests are able to add enjoyment to the cruise by participating more. All those aboard will appreciate the guest who is useful, doesn't injure the boat or crew, and helps contribute to a fine boating holiday. Want to be invited back?

— Barbara Bradfield

Let your boat of life be light, packed with only what you need — a homely home and simple pleasures, one or two friends, worth the name, someone to love and someone to love you, a cat, a dog, and a pipe or two, enough to eat and enough to wear, and a little more than enough to drink; for thirst is a dangerous thing.
　　　　　　　—Three Men in a Boat, Jerome K. Jerome

1
GETTING READY TO GO

So you are going on a boating holiday. You are thrilled and anticipate a great trip, but aren't sure what to pack. Whether the boat is 26 feet long or 126 feet long, power or sail, the same guidelines apply.

First, get a good idea of where you will be cruising and how long you will be out at sea. Find out if any special-event dressing will be required, but don't get carried away with clothing. Let simplicity and comfort be your packing guide.

Remember that there isn't any dirt on a boat, so even for young children it isn't necessary or practical to change outfits frequently. A few rules will ensure both creature comforts and another invitation to cruise.

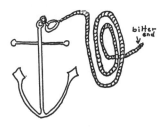

WASHING ON BOARD

While doing your hand washing, keep in mind that all boats have a limited water supply. If you are cruising in salt water, try using it for some of your laundering. Why salt water? No matter what size the boat and how much water she carries, it is a pain for the owners to spend time filling the tank in port when they would rather be off cruising. Save the tank water for showers and drinking. Using salt water for other needs is fun and easy. You can spend many a pleasant afternoon sitting on the swim step or perched on beach rocks giving smaller clothes, and sometimes dishes, a quick scrubbing. What an adventurous and virtuous way to get those chores done! (A word of advice here about drying your laundry: always tie or clothes-pin laundry securely to avoid having it disappear forever into the depths, the victim of a lifting breeze.) If you think using salt water seems peculiar, how about this: in the old days, sailors used urine to wash their hair and clothes when the water supply was low. That method of laundering got rid of their head lice and bleached the cloth, too. Urine also is said to help cure athlete's foot... It is a pretty grim suggestion for hygiene and one we hope need not be used, but remember...

**The Good Guest
ALWAYS
conserves water!**

Luggage

Thoughtful packing begins with luggage. Use only soft-sided luggage! Hard-sided bags, which are difficult to stow, will bang around noisily and be in the way. A duffel is ideal, but plastic sacks are fine, too. Assume that once aboard, your luggage will be stowed and no one will see it again until the end of the trip.

Keep in mind that your living space is smaller than what you are used to, and all non-essentials are a nuisance. (This includes packaging. Remember to contribute as little garbage and clutter to the boat as possible by discarding that box and bringing only the toothpaste tube.) Aside from essential toiletries necessary to your health and well-being, and suitable clothing, let your motto be "Travel Light!"

Clothes drying on boom

If you are heading out on a lengthy voyage, your hosts should have information about laundromats. Ration your clothing supply and do a little hand washing, too.

Clothing

Get information about heating systems on the boat and pay close attention to the season and location of your voyage. Before buying expensive gear, check to see if it might be available to borrow from the ship's locker. If you do buy rain gear, be advised that the cheap plastic stuff is not a good idea. You will be cold, miserable and wet when you need protection from the elements. Protect yourself from wind and rain and always, whatever the season, take long-johns. They don't take up much space, and they pay off greatly in comfort.

A good, though not essential, feature to consider about choosing boat-friendly pants: they should be a bit wide in the legs. It's nice to be able to roll them up so you can wade to the knee or keep the bottoms dry while hosing down the dinghy.

If traveling in warm weather, be sure to include a sun hat and appropriate shorts and T-shirts (and a bathing suit for the civilized places). Though a day might be warm, wind on the water can make the air chilly. Plan for adequate protection from the wind as well as the sun. Keep in mind the intensity of reflected light on the water and its ability to go up, in and around corners to find you. Take adequate sun screen.

> **SAILING DUDS**
>
> **The sailor's classic outfit is dungarees (jeans), shirt, sweater, wool cap, and deck shoes. The dungaree tradition began in the 18th century, when a coarse cloth from India called dungri came into use for ship's sails. Sailors used this durable material to make their own clothes and coated the cloth with tar to keep it weatherproof.**

Shoes

Now, for the feet. Forget about taking shoes with hard or black soles. Deck shoes may or may not be mandatory. They will keep you from slipping on the decks, but sneakers work equally well.

The Captain may request that you always wear shoes. This is not an attempt to cramp your style, but a sensible safety precaution. The decks are slippery! The cleats and chocks lie waiting to stub your toes! The Bad

Guest will race to a task, crack up against a deck box, sprain his or her foot, pitch over the side, cause undue delays while being fished out, and will have to spend the holiday in painful recovery! All this can be avoided by wearing shoes, moving carefully, and heeding the Captain.

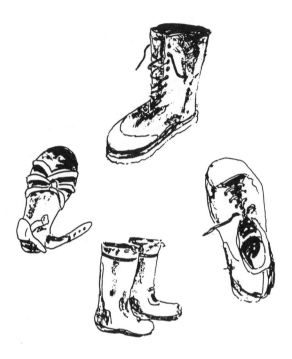

In addition to a pair of shoes for the boat, the Good Guest will have a pair of shoes or boots for the beach as well. Sport sandals are great for warm weather beach exploring and will protect your feet from jagged rocks, barnacles, oyster cuts, and other foot hazards.

One of the great pleasures of boating is exploring ashore, but it's important to be selective in choosing what comes back to the boat with you. Mud, stones, muck, leaves, excess sand and rotting seaweed are all better left on shore. Be certain to clean your shoes and yourself off thoroughly before boarding the dinghy and coming aboard the mother ship.

Always check for stones before re-boarding!

CLOTHING ESSENTIALS

Cold weather check list:

- sweater
- shirt
- pants
- wool cap
- soft-soled shoes
- jacket for wind and rain
- sweats/long-johns
- windbreaker

Warm weather check list:

- sun hat with chin strap
- sun screen
- beach shoes
- long and short-sleeved T-shirts
- bathing suit
- shorts
- soft-soled shoes
- beach shoes
- windbreaker

The thoughtful guest will find out if sheets and towels are provided. Find out if you should bring a sleeping bag.

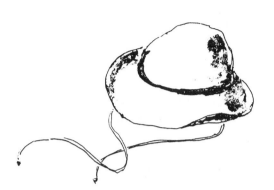

The Good Guest will anticipate and accept the fact that a boat will not have all the luxuries and conveniences of one's house. The best source of information about what to take, or leave at home, is your Captain or Mate. Don't be shy! Ask! It will be appreciated and, chances are, you will have more space for essentials.

Leave at home

- perfume - You are in close quarters and your fragrance will be unavoidable. One guest was so strongly doused that the boat's bedding had to be cleaned twice and the closets aired in her stateroom before we dared occupy it again.

- jewelry - If it goes overboard, it's really gone. If it tangles in the lines you could hurt yourself and feel like an idiot as well.

- small electric appliances (hairdryer, electric razor) -Take these only if the Captain says it is OK and it is practical to use them aboard. Remember that the ship's power is probably DC, not AC, which appliances run on.

DO NOT bring illegal drugs EVER. The Coast Guard does practice random boat searches. If illegal drugs are found, the boat will be seized!

Bring if possible

- sunglasses - They are essential to your eyes for coping with year-round water glare. Bring something to tie them on with! Glasses are almost impossible to retrieve when they go overboard.

- a small day pack for hikes and picnics.

- your own binoculars - The Captain is very particular about his personal, probably expensive binoculars, and expects them to be adjusted and always available. He will have little patience with the guest who is using them. Bring binoculars with a neck strap attached and be certain to put the strap around your neck! That way you will be ready for all the interesting sights while keeping your binoculars from sliding off the table and crashing to the deck.

While at anchor, an otherwise excellent guest took Barbara's binoculars out to the cockpit to watch for eagles. Guest set the binoculars on a small table, which was soon bumped. The binoculars crashed to the deck. They were now totally out of alignment and useless, unless there is a thrill in feeling like your eyeballs are being sucked out of the sockets. Barbara's husband fiddled with the binoculars, hoping for a lucky repair and to make Guest feel less badly. When this failed, he carefully dropped the binoculars onto the deck from the same height, facing down. All had a good laugh when this tactic seemed to work. The binoculars miraculously realigned and everyone felt much better. That repair job made a great story until two days after Guest's departure... when the binoculars again went completely out of whack. The point of this story? Don't mess with someone else's binoculars. Bring your own.

- a pocket knife - Attach it to a lanyard to tie to your belt loop.

- child-sized life jackets for your young children - Most boats carry only standard adult sizes, much too big to be comfortable and effective for a child.

- a chart of the area you will be visiting - You may find it interesting

how to set courses and track your journey as you go (see UNDERWAY, Charts). Mark this chart up as much as you wish, but never mark the ship's charts. The chart table is sacred ground and you will be thought of as a very bad guest if you touch or move the equipment on the chart table in any way.

Gifts

If you are wondering how to thank your hosts, a gift is always a nice idea and should be a welcome treat. Remember to keep the size of the boat in mind. Leave the extra packaging at home! If the gift is large, is there a way to fold, condense, or roll it up to stow it aboard while it's not in use?

Our suggestions for great gifts include:

- a game (we like Scrabble, dominoes, backgammon, cribbage, Trivial Pursuit)

- a useful utensil (an oyster knife, a bottle opener, a can crusher), coasters

- a sun shower (a black plastic bag with shower head attached)

- a flashlight

- special food (wine, chocolates and fresh fruit and vegetables provide a welcome treat)

> **HELPING WITH EXPENSES**
>
> If you have been cruising as a non-paying guest with boat-owner friends and want to contribute toward expenses, here are some things you might offer to pay enroute: outboard gas fill-ups, overnight marina moorage, a sack of groceries, a meal ashore. No owner ever minds an offer and with sensitive negotiation, you will be able to chip in on the tab. Ordinary cruising costs are not the big ticket items, but you may be concerned if you're asked to help refuel the boat's 1,000 gallon tank! At that point, mention that you have fish hooks in your pocket and can't get to your wallet.

- a magnifying glass for the Captain's chart table.

You can be creative and practical by giving:

- an oversized clipboard for using charts in the wind outside

- a large plastic envelope for charts in wet exposures (great for dinghy trips, fishing, beachcombing)

- some photos of the boat that you took and making them into postcards (copy centers do this) to present as a post-trip gift.

Journals

A great parting gift to share with hosts and guests would be a journal which you've brought on board to record the amusing and interesting details of your cruise. Present this at the end of the voyage.

You can include pencil sketches, pressed flowers, quotes from witty fellow passengers, bird, bear and whale sightings, ideas for cooking and eating. This journal is for fun, unlike the Captain's log, which is kept to record engine data, departure and arrival times, anchorages and other technical details pertinent to a well-run ship. Do not write in the Captain's log unless invited. Note: you can also record thoughts in the special section in the back pages of this book.

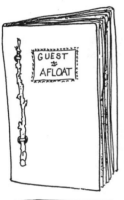

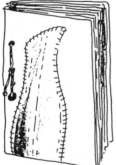

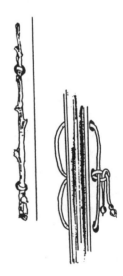

Sally's current journal is covered with fish skin, from a fish caught on a previous trip. To make the cover, sew, glue, or tie the dried skin on to sturdy cardboard (a cereal box is fine). Cut paper pages and a back cover to fit, and then make a simple binding. Poke two holes through the layers, feed a rubber band up through the holes and then insert a stick through the rubber band loops to fasten the book together. Or, poke three holes, and sew together with thread, twine, or yarn. Tie on shells, seaweed, moss, bangles to create a very unique, festive journal.

Welcome Aboard

On the next pages are two forms which may be photocopied and sent by the ship to the guests, and, a courtesy response by the guests.

Your Captain may send you these pertinent details before the cruise:

WELCOME ABOARD

_____
(Name of guest)

The _____
(boat name)

will depart on _____
(date)

at_____
(time)

Plan to board at_____

The _____ is_____feet long,
(boat name)

_____ feet wide and is powered by _____

She is a (type of boat)_____

On this trip she will carry _____ passengers

You will find the boat at

_____

_____

Our cruising schedule is

_____

_____

Your return date is _____at _____

It is useful for you to know ·

_____

_____

_____

Please bring

_____

_____

Our contact telephone number is

_____

The phone on the boat is

_____

The boat's call number for the marine operator is

_____

See you on the _____.

If there are any questions, please call me. Thank you

Signed,

_____

_____
Title

GUEST AFLOAT RESPONSE

My / Our transportation schedule to your boat is as follows:

I / we'll be there at

time _____date_____

A contact in case of emergency is

_____

who can be reached at _____

You should know that I / We are highly allergic to

_____

I/ We absolutely refuse to eat

_____

I/ We cannot live without _____

_____

(which you may or may not be able to supply)

I/ We will be celebrating a special occasion:

_____

These are the questions I/ we have about the boat or the cruising holiday:

_____

_____

Looking forward to the cruise!

Name (s) _____

Telephones : (Office)_____(Home)_____

(Office)_____(Home)_____

The steerage, in which I lived, was filled with coils of rigging, spare sails, old junk, and ship stores, which had not been stowed away. Moreover, there had been no berths put up for us to sleep in, and we were not allowed to drive nails to hang our clothes upon. The sea, too, had risen, the vessel was rolling heavily, and everything was pitched about in grand confusion."

Two Years before the Mast, *Richard Henry Dana*

2
TAKING THE TOUR:
WELCOME ON BOARD

It is crucial that you know the basic parts of the boat before you set foot on board. Imagine your embarrassment when the Captain tells you to stow your gear in the STARBOARD locker, proceed to the STERN and find your stateroom through the galley on the PORT side and your response is "HUH?" Understanding the terms BOW, PORT, STARBOARD, and STERN will make life go much more smoothly for all.

The special basic vocabulary is short, so learn it! When instructions are given to you and the crew, a quick and intelligent response is appreciated. When you report a concern to the person at the helm ("There is a deadhead off the starboard bow at one o'clock.") it is best to use the correct vocabulary and eliminate confusion.

BOW - the front of the boat. The area FORWARD is toward the BOW

STERN - the back of the boat

The area AFT is toward the STERN

Orient yourself by facing the BOW

PORT - the left side of the boat
(remember that you are facing the bow.)
Red, also a short word, is the color of
the running light on the port side (Say
to yourself, "Sailors drink red port!")
The words port and left both have four
letters (Say to yourself as you pull
away from the dock, "I just left port!"
or "Is there any red port left?")

STARBOARD - the right side of the boat.
The words starboard and right are long words.
Green, also a long word, is the color of the
running light on the starboard side.

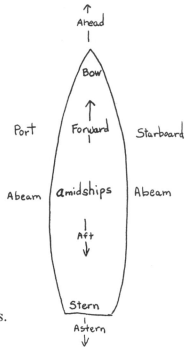

We have wondered about the origins of some of these terms and the answer to the evolution of PORT and STARBOARD surfaces. In ancient times, vessels had a steering board attached to one side (now known as the STARBOARD side) for maneuvering the boat. When the vessel docked in a port, the steering board had to be offshore, so the side next to the dock, the PORT side, was the one tied up.

Continuing the tour

Now that you have the ESSENTIAL words, here are more proper words which you will hear often and should use if you want to sound like an old salt: galley, saloon, head, stateroom, cockpit, bridge, and navigation station.

GALLEY - the kitchen

No mincing words here: the galley is the heart of the boat and the crew's

Galley area and stove with fiddles

morale is a reflection of how well they're fed. Nothing beats the tantalizing aroma of the next meal wafting up from the galley, and sea-going appetites are notoriously big. However, thoughtful guests explore the galley carefully, making sure that help is wanted and that they are not crowding the cook. Because the galley is a kitchen on the move, cutlery and dishes have special storage spaces; always notice what goes where and return items to their designated places. There are usually fiddle rails at counters and stovetop edges which help keep most things from sliding off, but they aren't foolproof. Keep in mind that there can be plenty of movement in the galley while tacking in a sailboat, or bouncing along on a rough sea under power, and it would be very unpleasant to drop a knife or dish on your foot. Some stoves are gimballed (pivoted mount) to keep the top level even when the boat heels (tips). This helps prevent the pots from toppling off except in really bad weather. Drawers and cupboards usually have a latch or special way of opening which keeps things from dumping out onto the deck during rough seas.

Remember to relatch or close doors securely.

Galleys, often very small spaces, produce remarkable quantities of food from many types of appliances and it's fun to see how the boat is equipped. Appliances may be as simple as those you would expect to use while camping, or as luxurious as those in your own house kitchen.

Operate the stove only after receiving special instruction from the captain or the crew. Stoves can be fueled by propane, alcohol, kerosene, diesel, electricity, or compressed natural gas; all have various pumps, valves, and different ways to ignite and operate. The electric range, which looks friendly, will most likely need the generator or shore power to work. Most boats have some kind of outdoor grill, which helps spread out the cooking area and gives a good excuse to sit around outside, enjoying the day while checking the coals and the meal.

Use of the cold compartment is pretty straightforward: when you open the door or lift the lid, be as efficient as possible and get it closed again soon. (Remember when your mother scolded you for hanging on the open refrigerator door while you selected a snack? Bad Guests still do this on boats.) On a boat it's important to keep the ice supply from melting and/or not drain power off the system, so avoid idly pawing through the boat's supplies while the cold escapes through the open door. Bigger boats have refrigerators which look like the ones at home, but remember the power drain and be quick about your business. Take care if you've been in a rough passage; the food can get very stirred up inside the refrigerator and might tumble out onto the deck when you open the door.

If you've drawn dish duty, there'll be a limited supply of fresh water. Hot water is not guaranteed, though on some boats water heats when the engines or generator runs. Even with a full sink system, learn to wash boating style, using less water and soap. Consider washing dishes in the lake or with sea water, then using fresh tank water for the final rinsing.

Many boaters prefer to use disposable paper and plastic rather than real dishes. Their decision is based on the amount of water the boat carries or their concern about breakage, but it also creates prodigious amounts of garbage, which is sometimes hard to dispose of while cruising. When dealing with garbage, always sort and compact it as directed. Never toss it overboard.

SALOON - the main cabin area, an inside gathering place

The saloon is a wonderful mix of function and charm. It's a good place for reading and writing, playing games and visiting. The furnishings could be multipurpose: lockers and stowage nooks are built into benches, seats and bulkheads; tables and sofas may convert to beds. In many boats, the saloon is the indoor eating area. It's important to keep this area picked up to avoid spills and falls when the crew hustles to a task.

Ship's kerosene lantern

The HEAD - toilet area

A marine toilet is different from what we are used to in our houses and requires thoughtful use. It will tolerate only human waste ("Put nothing in the bowl you haven't eaten.") and conservative amounts of toilet paper. Do not put any other paper products in the head. Unless you are far out in the ocean, the waste must go into a holding tank and be disposed of at a pump-out station. So keep in mind that each use fills up the tank a bit more and that the tank's holding capacity is finite. The Captain will have to get to a pump-out station when the tank is full.

Each boat may have a different system, so it is helpful to learn the necessary steps to use the marine toilet. You may be hand pumping, pushing a button, pressing a pedal or doing those in combination. The main types of marine toilets include mechanical, electric (operated by pressing a button), vacu-flush (like on an airplane), and even a basic bucket.

Marine toilets often have a small pedal at the base of the bowl, which must be pressed to flush water through as the waste exits. In order to finish off the waste's trip through the pipes to the tank, it may be necessary to press the pedal a little longer, or give a few more strokes to the lever.

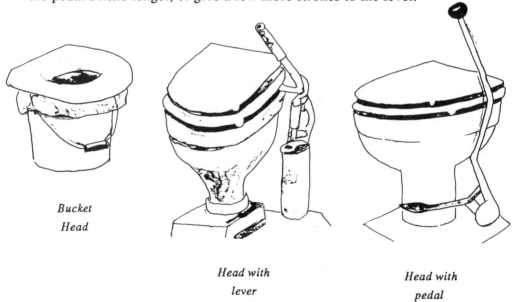

Bucket
Head

Head with
lever

Head with
pedal

It's always a good idea to put the lid down after use. This prevents things from falling in if the boat is rolling around a bit while you are underway. Your Captain and Mate are the best source of instructions for head use. ASK!

A word about ablutions in the head. You will most likely take care of your teeth, face, shaving, showers and shampooing in the head. Water usage must be as constant a consideration as avoiding debris when you are at the helm. Conserve water at all times. Be thoughtful and plan ahead! Turn off the faucet when your toothbrush is in your mouth! Turn off the faucet before you reach for your towel!

The water pump is a dead give-away. You may think no one will know how much water you are using, but it's hard for the Captain and Mate to avoid hearing the thump-thump-thump of the pump as the Bad Guest indulges in hedonistic water use. If you are lucky enough to have a shower, learn to enjoy taking one boat-style: get wet and turn off the water, soap up, then turn the water on to rinse. If you are careful this way, you'll get to take more showers during the trip.

Ship's sink in head area

STATEROOM - the bunk area or private sleeping quarters

Bunk area

It is a delicious feeling to snuggle down into your bunk on a boat. This is usually a cozy space, yours for the time you are sleeping, so be flexible if there are space limitations and enjoy its uniqueness. Everything you'll need is close at hand: a reading light (whether it is your own flashlight or a permanent fixture attached to the bulkhead), your reading material, extra clothes perhaps in the hanging locker or a small drawer, and fresh air drifting in through the open port.

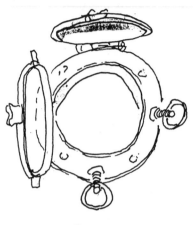

Open port

A port is an opening in the hull to admit light and air. The glass used in the port to keep the hull watertight is termed a portlight if it can be opened, and a deadlight if it cannot.

The hull configuration of a sailboat generally makes the space below deck more compact. Your bunk may be converted between dinner and breakfast from a couch to a bed. The interior in a sailboat is likely to be darker, cosier and more intimate.

It's important to keep your sleeping area ship-shape. A good routine is to tidy up the area upon rising, stow and secure all gear to keep things from rolling around and falling about, close the port against incoming sea water while underway and secure all doors firmly to avoid banging sounds.

COCKPIT - outdoor area

In both sailboats and powerboats, the cockpit is an outdoor area normally near the stern. The transom, which encloses the stern, may have a gate (transom door) to give access to the swim step or to get down to the dinghy. It is a pleasant fair weather gathering place.

You will spend much of your cruising time in a sailboat's cockpit. Here are the tiller or wheel, engine controls, navigation equipment, lots of sheets, winches, and cleats and built-in seats to entice you to find your spot and relax. The seats usually contain storage for lines, life jackets and other gear, so be ready to move aside. The action can be fast-paced while sailing, and the boat will heel, so be sure to move carefully to avoid injury. Pay attention to your can of pop and plate of food to avoid a mess. If you are clueless about the business end of sailing, stay out of the way until someone gives you a job to do.

The cockpit on a powerboat, if it has one, is normally aft of the saloon on the same deck level. Often the cockpit is a perfect spot for outdoor leisure activity, similar to what you would expect of a patio. Sometimes, especially on fast boats, the cockpit is noisy and smelly from exhaust when underway. Many powerboats use the cockpit for fishing and you may see a fighting chair and a set of controls for the engine and steering.

BRIDGE - the control station

Controls for operating powerboats are generally located in one or, sometimes, two places: the wheelhouse, the flying bridge (usually shortened to "flybridge") or the steering station. The wheelhouse, if the boat has one, is usually located up and forward of the saloon. It is an indoor area separate from the galley, saloon and staterooms and contains the equipment associated with navigation. Smaller cruisers often have steering stations which are a part of the main cabin area. Steering controls are also up on the flybridge. Originally intended as an elevated platform for spotting fish, it is now most often a popular outdoor place to operate the boat. Not all of the navigation equipment is there unless the flybridge is the main control station.

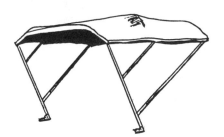

Overhead, a collapsible canvas bimini gives protection from the sun.

Bimini top

NAVIGATION STATION - here you'll find navigating equipment used to get to a destination

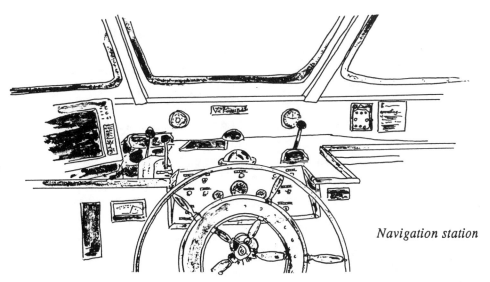

Navigation station

Compass

The COMPASS is a major navigational aid. Without it, one would have a heck of a time getting from here to there. Along with a chart and a pencil, the compass enables a skipper to head in the right direction, know where the boat is enroute, and navigate in fog and in unknown waters. All boaters using power or sail should understand the basic fundamentals of reading and using the compass.

(See UNDERWAY: "At the Wheel" for details on reading the compass.)

You will notice that the Captain and Mate spend a lot of time fiddling with their CHARTS. Charts are filled with information crucial to traveling safely and successfully by boat to a destination. They show natural and man-made features on the water that you can use to help keep track of where you are.

Charts give important details of safe channels and of hazards to navigation. They indicate depth of water, rocks to avoid, harbors for tying up and anchoring out, what terrain to expect and how far it is between places. Never mark the Captain's chart without permission. The little doodle you absent-mindedly write on the chart may be confusing and distracting to the navigator.

You may also note an array of electronic paraphernalia at the boat's navigation station. Although they may appear to be hopelessly complicated, fancy toys, electronics can be a great help in navigating, in confirming one's old-fashioned calculations, and providing a safety cushion of information to all aboard. In case you are curious about the electronics, we offer a brief run-down on those most likely to be there. Because gadgets constantly change and there are so many types, be sure to ask your Captain for instructions before punching buttons.

GPS, or Global Positioning System, tells you exactly where you are in the world. Satellites are used to give exact latitude and longitude coordinates. The screen can also show the boat's course, speed, distance traveled, ETA (estimated time of arrival) to destination, where the Man Overboard hit the water and a multitude of other remarkable pieces of information. Ask for the instruction manual, study up on it and see if you can drop a few gems of enlightenment in the wheelhouse.

RADAR visually displays the land and solid objects surrounding you. You are the dot at the center of the screen. The circles emanating from you (the boat) represent specific distances. Radar is invaluable in the fog and while running at night.

DEPTH SOUNDERS show the distance in feet, meters or fathoms between the bottom of the boat and the sea floor. This is crucial information when coming into a harbor or anchoring. The Good Guest might offer to call out depths when the Captain heads into a particularly tricky spot.

VHF is the special radio-telephone used for communication. Unlike a CB or regular house telephone, the VHF radio is not a place for superfluous conversation or chit chat. Special procedures are used when calling (see SAFETY for details), and care must be taken to keep calls short: no more than three minutes except for safety calls. It is possible to contact

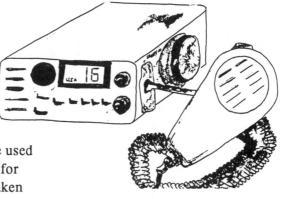

VHF radio

someone ashore using the VHF by calling the Marine Operator. Your Captain will have information on this.

Many powerboats and sailboats have an AUTOPILOT. The autopilot steers the boat automatically and continuously along a preset compass course. Its benefit is to free up the helmsman to tend to other navigating tasks while underway. It has a "dodge" control to override the system temporarily for immediate manual operation when, for example, a log needs to be avoided.

Sometimes boats have lots more equipment. We feel the rest of it should lie in wait for you dauntless souls who love electronics and get a charge out of learning about gadgets. Keep in mind that all of these tools can fail, but charts won't. Electronics are supplements to navigating and should be valued for contributing information rather than giving the absolute answer to every question. Good luck to you!

There is nothing so quiet as a boat when the motor has stopped; it seems to lie with held breath. One gets to longing for the deep beat of the cylinders."
Sea Of Cortes, John Steinbeck and Edward Ricketts

3
GETTING ORIENTED
TO YOUR BOATING WORLD

Things That Power The Boat

Let's be frank here. That romantic "deep beat of cylinders" is not exactly what comes to mind after hearing the engine during a long day's cruise. Is there anything as odious as the incessant whine of a sailboat's auxiliary, the loud hoarse-voiced powerboat engines, the inescapable throb and clamor of whatever it is powering the boat? We've all experienced the relief when the engine was shut-down and sighed, "Ah!"

But the next day we are happy to fire it up again in order to continue our adventure, blessing the machine for running smoothly and on command. The noise of some boats is worse than others, so you might want to include earplugs in your gear to get a break from its noise.

Almost all boats, whatever their design or size, have some sort of an engine. We'll take a look at powerboat engines and sailboats with auxiliaries first. Curious about engines and what type powers the boat? Read on.

Engines

These are the basic types of propulsion: outboards, inboard/ outboards and inboards. There can be combinations of one or two engines in all of these types and they are fueled by either gas or diesel.

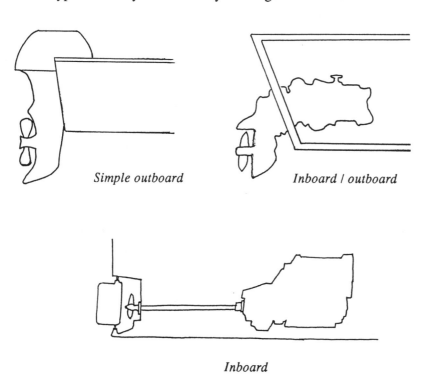

Simple outboard   *Inboard / outboard*

Inboard

If you are helping to fill the fuel tanks, be certain that you are putting the correct fuel in the right tank. Always read the fill cap carefully to avoid putting fuel in the water tank or water in the fuel tank. This is not an amusing mistake for a guest to make.

Unlike cars, which have a radiator to cool the engine, boat engines are cooled by sea water. Cars have several forward gears; boats have only one. Particular care is taken to ventilate the compartment of gas engines before starting the engine to avoid the chance of an explosion. The Captain always takes a strong sniff, sampling the air for fumes, and turns on the blower before starting. Use of a blower is not necessary with diesel engines.

Batteries

Larger cruising boats have a set of batteries to do all the electrical work. These are called "house" batteries and run the lights and DC appliances. Be aware that there is a limited capacity available from these batteries, so lights and other "juice drainers" should not be left on unnecessarily. Always turn out lights not in use, suggest candles at dinner, and have a flashlight by your bunk for nighttime excursions. The batteries can be charged by running the main engine or, when plugged in, to shore power through the battery charger. There is usually a separate battery for starting the engine.

AC Power

In order to produce AC power, the boat will either have a genset or an inverter. The genset consists of an engine and a generator that makes AC power. The inverter is an electrical device which converts DC current out of the house battery into AC. This is a limited capacity and it does draw down the house battery when being used to make AC. But the inverter is great because you can use the outlets for small appliances and make toast and coffee without turning on the noisy generator to do it.

Check with the Captain about using small appliances like hair dryers and electric shavers to make sure the boat's system can handle it.

Here are details on this boat's power plant: (Skipper or owner fills this in)

_____

_____

_____

Sailing

If you are on a sailboat, it's a good idea to know the basics of powering the boat by wind power, especially if you may be asked to get up there and help. Using this knowledge will make your boating environment safer and you will learn sailing techniques more quickly and with less confusion.

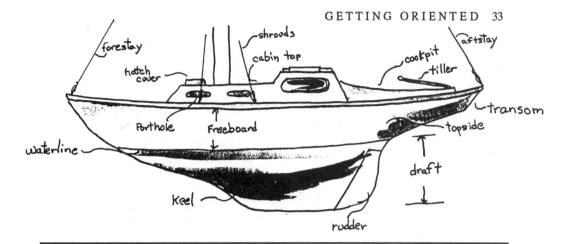

Sailboats have five main parts: hull, sails, mast, rudder, and centerboard or keel.

A wet sheet and a following sea,
A wind that follows fast,
And fills the white and rustling sail,
And bends the gallant mast.
The Songs of Scotland *(1825), Allan Cunningham*

Sailing terms

BATTEN - a small, stiff piece of wood or plastic inserted to keep the sail's shape

BOOM - a horizontal spar attached to bottom of sail, so named for the sound it makes when it cracks into your head if you forget to duck

CLEW - the rear corner of a sail

HALYARD - a line to hoist a sail

JIB - a smaller triangular sail forward of mainsail

MAINSAIL - the primary, or largest sail

MAST- a vertical spar to hold up sails

RUDDER - a board in the water attached to the stern used for steering the boat

SHEETS - lines used to control sails

SHROUDS - supporting wires from the mast to sides of the boat

STAYS - a wire from the mast to the bow and/or to the stern

TELLTALES - little bits of material tied up on the rigging which flutter in the wind to show which way the wind is blowing

TILLER - a lever that is fixed to and controls the rudder. Note: if you push the tiller to the left, the bow turns right. The stern swings out when turning, so leave room if you are departing from a dock or are close to another boat. Remember, too, that a boat steers from its back end — not front (like a bicycle).

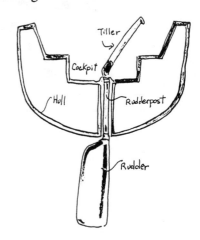

Stern of boat showing tiller

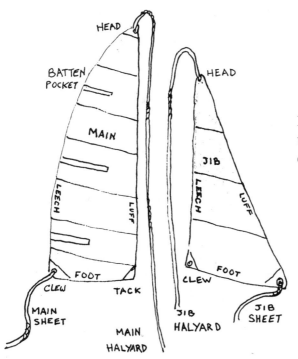

Sails with vocabulary

Learn this small rhyme
to know the edges
of the sails:

> *Head aloft*
> *Foot below*
> *Luff before*
> *and leach in tow.*

Sailboats have a fin projecting down from the bottom of the boat which keeps the boat from slipping sideways. These keels are one of three main types:

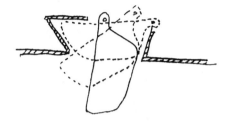

Centerboard - a retractable plate that extends below the bottom of the boat. This can be raised or lowered.

Centerboard

Daggerboard - This type of keel can be raised or lowered (like a dagger in a sheath).

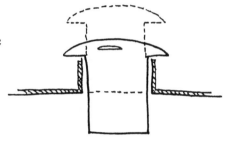

Daggerboard

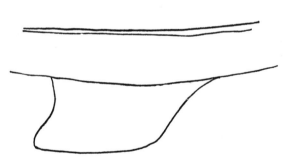

Fixed keel - A permanent part of the bottom of the boat. It resists sideways motion of the boat.

Fixed keel

Warning

Know what your draft is (the depth of the boat extending below the water line) and always remember it. You need this information to avoid unplanned contact with the bottom!

Points of sailing

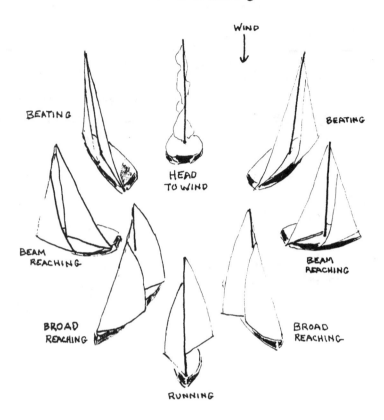

Eye of wind - where the wind is coming from

Beating - sails are close hauled

Beam reaching - sheets are eased out

Broad reaching - sheets are eased out further

Running - sheets are fully out and the wind is from the stern

Tacking - beating to windward, steering a zig-zag course

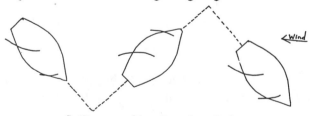

Sailboat tacking into the wind

Coming about - the bow turning through the eye of the wind and putting the wind on the other side of the boat. Let the jib's sheet go when the jib starts to luff, take it in on the other side as it fills. Correct your course.

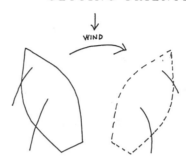

Sailboat coming about

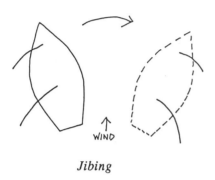

Jibing

Jibe - turning the stern of the boat through the eye of the wind (the boom may swing around fast here, so watch your head.)

Windward - the direction from which the wind blows

Leeward - (pronounced "loo erd") away from the direction of the wind

Luffing - to come toward the wind and relieve pressure on the sails (the sail looks loose and bumpy)

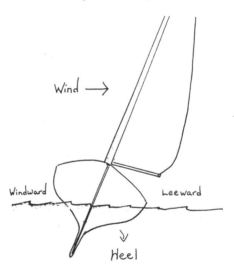

Windward, leeward

Sailboat Hardware

Shackle

Cam cleat

Turnbuckle

Pulley

Things to remember

- Have everything ready before you cast off from the mooring or dock

- Know which way the wind is blowing (see the telltales, hold your wet finger up and feel the wind on your face)

- Be sure that the sheets are free to run and all gear is stowed

- If you are on a small boat, distribute your weight as evenly as possible

- Pull in the sheet until the sail just fills

- Say "Ready about" when ready to come about

- Say "Helms alee" when pushing the tiller well down to leeward to come about

- Watch for the boom

- Remove the winch handles when not in use (these are on bigger boats)

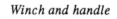

- If the winds are too strong, reduce sail, let the sheet out or point into the wind

Winch and handle

- When docking or returning to the mother ship, if possible approach into the wind.

Furling sails

All hands can help furl the sails at the end of the day. Furling is a seamanlike way of securing the sails; the idea is to fold the sail neatly in place on the top of the boom. After the sail is furled, the mainsail is always covered to protect the sail from the sun and to keep it dry. The mainsail is held in place on the boom with strips of cloth or pieces of line (these are called stops or gaskets), or a shock cord stretched between hooks on the sides of the boom and zig-zagged over the top of the folded sail.

Smaller sails are stored in special sail bags.

There are four steps in furling a sail

1. Insert the stops (gaskets) between the boom and the sail. Space and tie them evenly.

2. Lower the mainsail.

3. Furl the sail on the boom in smooth folds neatly arranged, with no wrinkles.

4. Secure the folds with the stops. (Cross the ends over the sail, then under the boom and back up to the top of the folded sail to be tied firmly.)

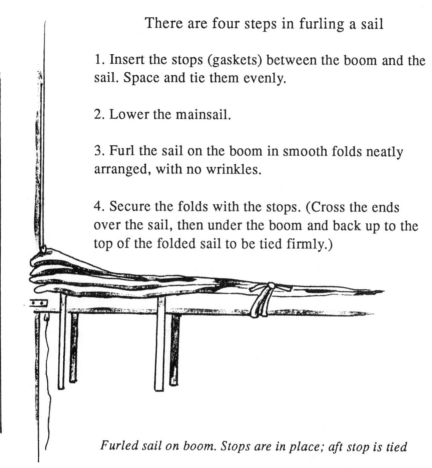

Furled sail on boom. Stops are in place; aft stop is tied

Sometimes the sail will be bundled around, rather than folded upon the top of, the boom. It is then secured with a marling hitch.

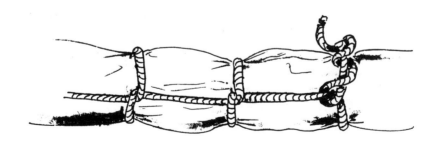

Sail furled and tied with marling hitch

SMALL CRAFT SAILING

You might also have an opportunity to sail on a small sailboat, sometimes carried on board larger craft. Each boat handles differently and has a different combination of sails and sheets. Instructions are boat-specific, but to give you a rough idea of what you might experience in a 12- foot Ranger sailing dinghy, here is a sailing scenario:

I have noted the weather and told the Captain I'm heading out for a sail. Before I leave, I check to see that I have a life jacket and all that gear is stowed. The day is clear and sunny with a light, steady breeze.

Good advice runs through my mind as I cast off and climb in: move carefully, keep low, sit down quickly in the center. The sheets for the mainsail and jib are rigged and clear, the centerboard set, and the tiller ready and free to maneuver. I note the wind direction, head slightly off the wind until the sails fill and get underway.

The mainsail fills nicely and then I sheet in the jib for more speed. I skim along smoothly, feeling the sun on my face, hearing the whisper of the hull cut through the water, and experiment to see what the boat will do. I glance up constantly into the sail to see that there is no unwanted luffing, check the telltales for wind direction and make necessary adjustments.

I tack up the bay, using the anchored boats as a zig-zag course. I admit to a little flutter of panic when the Ranger heels too far, but know I can move to the windward side or let out the sheets in order to return the boat immediately to a more sedate angle.

I eventually make my way back to the mother ship, the "big" boat, coming up on her stern. I approach deliberately and slowly, heading into the wind. With good use of the tiller and letting go of the mainsail and jib sheets at the right moment, I can and do dock safely.

I lower and secure the sails, carefully disembark and tie my little sailboat up securely.

Give me a spirit that on this life's rough sea
Loves t' have his sails filled with a lusty wind,
Even till his sail-yards tremble, his masts crack,
And his rapt ship run on her side so low
That she drinks water, and her keel plows air.
—The Conspiracy of Charles, Duke of Byron,
George Chapman (1608)

Types of sailboats

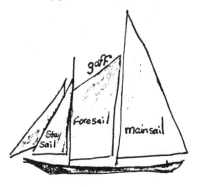

Schooner
Two or more masts with the aftermast tallest

Ketch
*Two masted, aftermast shorter
and foreward of the rudder*

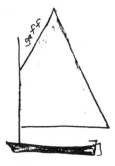

Catboat
*Gaff-rigged, simplified
handling --- popular workboat*

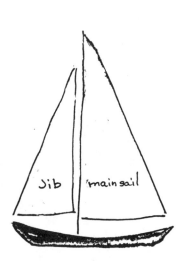

Sloop
*Single masted with a mainsail
and a jib*

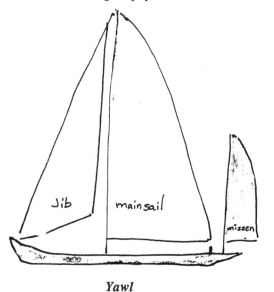

Yawl
*Two-masted sailboat, the shorter mast
after the rudder*

Passage, immediate passage! the blood burns in my veins!
Away O soul! hoist instantly the anchor!
Cut the hawsers - haul out - shake every sail!
Have we not stood here like trees in the
ground long enough?
Have we not groveled here long enough, eating
and drinking like mere brutes?"
— *Leaves of Grass*, Walt Whitman

4

UNDERWAY

When the anchor has been weighed (lifted) or the lines cast off and the boat has no connection with the land, you are officially underway. Being underway is uniquely different from other travel experiences: you and your fellow voyagers are isolated, dependent on each other and the Captain's good judgment for your safety.

Some guests may have a flutter of unease, recollecting Captain Bligh. But generally, if all maintain a spirit of cooperation and goodwill, mutiny is unnecessary. Remember that the Captain is responsible for your safety, the safety of the boat, and for decisions made while underway. Don't panic! Captain Bligh is dead.

The Perfect Captain

After many years' observation and reflection, we note that the perfect Captain will:

- speak quietly and clearly
- give explicit instructions
- be sober and alert
- see humor in situations
- keep an even temper
- never swear at the crew
- listen to this list if it's necessary.

The Perfect Guest

You, the guest, also have responsibilities. You are always aware of others' activity on the boat and sit down or stand back rather than be underfoot. You may ask some questions, but not too many. You might volunteer to wash windows, swab the decks, polish the brass, help watch for logs, and even clean the heads! (You get bonus guest points for this one.) Whether you are off duty or on duty, it is important that you always will:

- avoid blocking the Captain's view
- resist messing with the charts and bridge instruments
- report peculiar sightings, smells, and noises
- be aware that all loud noises make the Captain's heart stop
- open and close the port holes at appropriate times.
- stow gear and tidy up
- avoid standing in the companionways

Should you be invited to participate actively while underway:

Companionway

- volunteer to help stand watch
- offer to check the oil, gauges etc.

- ask questions if your task is not clear
- act only on the Captain's signal

If rough seas are expected, be ready to help prepare the boat. All loose items must be stowed, some things should be tied down, towels may be stuffed in between the dishes and glasses, and find out what and where the sea-sick prevention kit is.

> **If you are down in the engine room or up on the top deck with a mental lapse on which way to turn a valve, remember this to loosen or tighten the knob as needed:**
>
> **"Leftie, loosie. Rightie, tightie."**

Both powerboats and sailboats are affected by waves, wind and wakes. Depending on her size and the condition of the seas, a powerboat will bounce and roll in the water. Sailboats heel (lean) when sailing. You will get used to this natural (and unavoidable) action. Always remember that surfaces will not remain horizontal: think about where you place your coffee cup, your soup, and your feet to avoid slips and spills.

If you see a log, deadhead, or any other object in the boat's path, let the helmsperson know about it in a predetermined way ("See the log just off the starboard bow" or "See the deadhead at 10 o' clock," for example). You might point to it, too.

The helm's response should be, "Thank you." Be calm, be observant, be aware that if YOU have the helm and are unsure about what to do when a tricky situation looms, you can always slow the boat down!

Deadheads: danger in the water

Knots

While underway, you will have time to learn some important boating skills. One of your first priorities should be mastering several often-used knots. You can then more ably help with docking and casting off, dinghy tending, fender hanging, and the thousands of little jobs that continuously come up requiring an appropriate knot for the task. Be patient as you attempt to learn these knots. You will get many chances to try them out, which is a good thing. Expect to need a refresher course for each voyage. We find that we always must rehearse the knots to revive our skills if we've been ashore too long. The most commonly used special knots are illustrated. These knots will never jam or work loose on their own, and will always be easy to untie. Each knot has a typical purpose.

The most important knot is the BOWLINE (pronounced boh-lyn). This is a wonderful knot, always useful and easy to do once you've memorized it. It does not slip or jam, and is sometimes called the king of knots. Its uses are endless: fenders, dock lines, dinghy painter to mother ship, bucket over the side, clothesline between davits, etc.

Bowline

The SHEET BEND is used to tie two lines of different thickness together. This is useful if you need a longer line quickly. For example, you notice the line is too short for assisting with a tow, so connect appropriate lines with the SHEET BEND to get additional length.

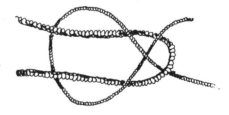

Sheet bend

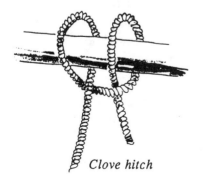

The CLOVE HITCH is used to secure a line to a rail. Fenders and dinghy painters are tied with the CLOVE HITCH.

Clove hitch

The FISHERMAN'S BEND is used to make fast to a ring. It consists of two round turns on the ring and two half hitches around the standing part of the line. It's also called the BUCKET HITCH, as it is used for tying a line to a bucket.

Fisherman's bend

To MAKE FAST TO A CLEAT, make one complete turn around the cleat going clockwise or counter clockwise depending on the entrance of the line, then at least two figure eights. Cleats come in many different sizes and shapes, but the formula remains the same.

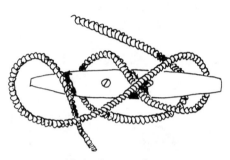

Make fast to cleat

The FIGURE OF EIGHT KNOT, or STOPPER KNOT, is used by sailors to prevent a sheet from running out of a block.

Figure eight

Bear in mind that even if you have efficiently tied the appropriate knot, the Captain still may redo it. This is no reflection on your knot, but on his/her compulsion to retie and adjust sometimes for the hell of it. Consider your knot task successful if you have secured the boat to the dock when the crucial moment comes. If you have forgotten the appropriate knot, just secure as best you can and stand by until it gets retied.

Once on the dock, secure your lines as quickly as possible.

There are many excellent knot books. We recommend *The Klutz Book of Knots*, by John Cassidy, for practice. It includes good drawings, a piece of string, and holes in the book to tie the knots.

When you have perfected these important knots, continue on and learn some decorative ones. In olden times, fancy work was a source of pride and competition for the sailors and an important part of their leisure time activity. The goal in fancy work is to master a variety of knots and have them uniformly finished. Sailors made handles for tools, rope ladders, needle cases, string bags, table mats, rugs, necklaces, baskets, jar covers,

bellpulls, bracelets and quirts all worked in various sizes and colors. A wonderful fancy work book is *The Marlinspike Sailor* by Hervey Garrett Smith. You might make a handsome bell pull or fashion the TURK'S HEAD into napkin rings.

Turk's head knot

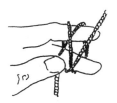  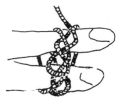 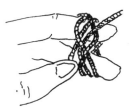

Hold standing end with thumb, go around fingers twice. Keeping to the right, continue following over and under until you have a three-strand knot. Take out the slack and cut off the ends underneath.

It's great fun to have knot tying competitions. Work for speed and accuracy, the usual requirements for jobs on the boat, and figure that when you can tie all the knots behind your back, you've about mastered it!

Leaving and Weighing Anchor

Time to get underway. Get aboard before the boat moves to avoid having to leap. Stand by to assist, but keep out of the others' way, for leaving the dock can have some exciting moments. Weighing anchor can be interesting, too, so it's best to be alert in case there is a snag in an otherwise predictable routine.

When leaving the dock, cast off lines only at the Captain's signal. Stand by to tend the dinghy, bring the fenders on board when well away, secure, coil and stow all lines if so directed. You might be asked to let the dinghy line out to trailing length behind the boat. Be careful the line does not drag over varnished wood.

Coiling a line

If you are asked to bring the fenders on board, take it seriously. These are the white cushions hanging on the side of the boat, protecting the hull from the dock. We admit to one or two rare, mortifying lapses when we've forgotten to haul in the fenders. It made our boats look sloppy and as if the crew didn't care.

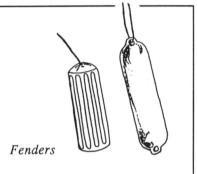

Fenders

Weighing anchor

Weighing anchor should be a simple process. The Captain provides slack in the rode (the anchor line) by slowly proceeding in the direction of the anchor until the rode is vertical. The crew hauls in the anchor by using the winch and/or windlass or hand over hand.

When the anchor becomes free of the bottom, this is known as "Anchor's aweigh!" Be prepared to help clean the rode and anchor as it comes up. Sometimes disgusting amounts of muck and seaweed have been keeping the anchor company and are not wanted on the boat. Sing this chantey while you haul up the anchor rode:

> *Oh Shenandoh, I love thy daughter.*
> *Heave away, I'm bound to go*
> *Across the wide Missouri.*

Sung in unison to a rhythm, the chantey will make work go faster and more smoothly. Sometimes.

What to Do While Cruising

Once the day is launched and you are settled in for a day of cruising, plan to have a few activities ready to amuse yourself. Projects which don't take up much space and can be contained in your immediate area might include:

- reading
- knot work
- crossword puzzles
- painting
- carving
- writing
- drawing
- bread making
- yoga stretches
- knitting
- listening to books on tape with your Walkman
- photographing
- maintaining a special cruising journal

Attitude is important while underway. "There is nothing so desperately monotonous as the sea, and I no longer wonder at the cruelty of pirates," wrote James Russell Lowell in *Fireside Travels 1864 At Sea*. Amuse yourself and do not expect to be entertained.

When the weather is disappointing or board games and hobbies have lost their attraction, the Good Guest might organize a Christmas-in-August party. It's great fun to draw names and make a present out of material on hand for a gift exchange. A shell necklace, walking stick, funny sculpture or carved clay may become the best gift that person has ever received. If imagination and enthusiasm are still going strong, require all to come to dinner in fancy dress (this may mean your last clean T-shirt with a seaweed bow tie!).

On some boats, life aboard is pleasantly paced by the chiming of the ship's clock. Guests puzzle over what the bells mean. You will notice that the bells ring eight times at 4 o'clock, 8 o'clock, and 12 o'clock. These are the hours that the crew traditionally changed WATCH. At 4:30, 8:30, and 12:30 one bell chimes, and at each half hour an additional bell will ring until a total of eight is reached and another WATCH begins. For example, 5 o'clock is two bells, 5:30 is three bells, 6 o'clock is four bells, and so on.

Kids Afloat

Children are wonderful to have aboard. They give everyone a good excuse to play and they often spot interesting things that are otherwise overlooked. If you are lucky enough to include children on a boat trip, there are many good activities which will be fun for everyone. With planning, neither you nor the kids will suffer from the restricted space.

Activities for kids

They might make their own postcards: gather seaweed, place a wet layer on heavy paper. When dry, the seaweed will be attached and the card can be sent to a friend, who will no doubt wonder over the mysterious, attractive texture. Beautiful postcards also can be made by painting the horizon, and adding in islands, bays, boats and peaks from looking at the chart or your surroundings as a reference.

It's messy, but fun, to carve soap bars (use Ivory for best results), or work with playdough. (A batch of playdough will keep very well in a covered coffee can. Mix 1 cup flour, 1/2 cup salt, 1 t cream of tartar, 1 cup water with a drop or two of food coloring if desired, and 2 T oil. Stir over heat until it forms a ball. Knead until smooth.)

It should be a real thrill for them, and you, to sight whales. Whales must be treated with respect: your Captain will travel parallel to them and approach no closer than 100 yards. Also, watch for porpoise. Those incredible creatures love to play tag in the boat's bow wave and sometimes will swim with you for miles.

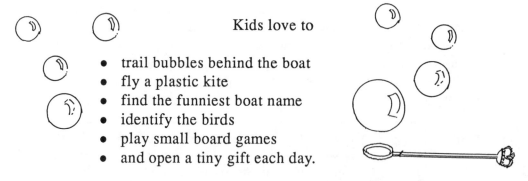

Kids love to

- trail bubbles behind the boat
- fly a plastic kite
- find the funniest boat name
- identify the birds
- play small board games
- and open a tiny gift each day.

Children and adults will quickly learn an important rule for life aboard:

ONE HAND FOR YOURSELF
ONE HAND FOR THE BOAT

Even in protected and calm water, a sudden wave or change in heading can surprise you. Keep one hand free to hold onto a railing for balance while moving about on the boat. The advantage to this balancing act is that it takes energy. This will counteract the relative lack of exercise and the extra amounts of great cruising food you will be enjoying (let's face it, these are boating realities).

Recipes Afloat

Have all the activities worked up your appetite? Eat and rejoice! Succumb to one of the notoriously gratifying highlights of cruising! Better yet, since you might have some extra time, put it to good use by baking bread or concocting a truly memorable dish for all to enjoy.

It is immensely satisfying to rustle up snacks and meals for a hungry crew, so we've included a few of our favorite galley recipes. We like to take advantage of foods from the sea and berries and herbs from forages ashore to add fresh ingredients to recipes whenever possible. Experience has shown, however, that it's also best to have decent backup with dried and canned staples in case a grocery stop is not possible. Our recipes are restricted to those with ingredients that are probably on hand, do not require refrigeration, have a long shelf life, taste fine either processed or fresh, do not have a delicate construction (in case the boat goes whap whap unexpectedly) and are just plain delicious! Most Mates appreciate an offer to take over the cooking for a meal; the thoughtful guest brings ingredients along if a special dish is planned.

Focaccia

Focaccia is excellent as an hors d'oeuvre, as a sandwich bread and as an accompaniment to an entree. Fortunately, this recipe makes two large, round 12-inch loaves — plenty for all to enjoy. Put it to rise in the warm engine room. This will keep it safe from crew taking tiny pinches to taste-test the dough.

Dissolve 3 T yeast in 2 cups warm water. Add 2 T sugar, 4 T olive oil, 1/3 cup salad oil, and 2 t salt. Gradually add up to 5 1/2 cups flour, knead at least 10 minutes until smooth. Place in a greased bowl and let rise, covered, twice. Punch down in the bowl after each rising. Grease two 12-inch round pizza sheets and divide the dough between the two. Use your greased fingers to press the dough out to the edges of the pans; cover and let rise for about 30 minutes. Meanwhile, mix 2 T olive oil with 2 cloves minced garlic and let stand. When the dough is ready to bake, brush on the oil and garlic mixture and sprinkle on a little rosemary, oregano, thyme or basil for topping. Bake at 375 degrees for about 30 minutes.

Cut the freshly baked focaccia into small wedges to present with these appetizer butters as a spread:

Raving Olive Butter

Mix a small can of chopped black olives with 1 T lemon juice (bottled is fine), 1 t minced garlic, 1/2 small container of chopped anchovies, and 2 T Parmesan cheese.

Tamer Olive Butter

Or, if anchovies are not acceptable and you have a supply of perishable condiments, mix 1/2 cup chopped black olives with 1/2 cup chopped green olives, 2 T butter, 1 t Dijon mustard, 1 t mayonnaise, and a dash of lemon juice.

Sandwiches

Slice the baked focaccia through the middle to make two circles and drizzle with olive oil. Sparingly, layer salami (the vacuum-packed kind keeps for a long time), sliced tomatoes or canned pimento, sliced canned marinated artichoke hearts, a bit of red onion rings, thin slices of white cheese and a sprinkling of grated Parmesan cheese and herbs such as basil, oregano and parsley over one half of the sliced focaccia. Place the other half on top and cut into sandwich portions. This creation is obviously one you can adapt to whatever supplies you may have on hand.

Fish Chowder

Fish chowder is an excellent way to make use of the day's catch. Even a small fish contributes a lot to round out a good soup, so keep the little (but legal) guys to add to the pot. The fish/shellfish additions are all best if fresh, but the broth is made quickly from canned ingredients.

In a large soup pot, saute 1/2 minced onion and 2 cloves garlic in 1 T olive oil. Add one 16 oz. can chopped tomato pieces, one 8 oz. can tomato sauce, 1 cup dry white wine, 3 T parsley, 1 t salt, 1/2 t each oregano and basil and 1 T diced chili peppers. Bring to a boil, reduce heat, then cover. Simmer for 20 minutes. Cut one pound or so of cleaned fish into pieces, removing all bones, and add to cooked broth. Simmer 5 minutes. Add 1/2 pound shrimp and 1 pound fresh steamer clams and simmer an additional 5 minutes, covered, until clams are well opened. Serves 4

East-West Comfort Soup

Not only nourishing, but beautiful! The ingredients are honest old pals which combine well to make a truly memorable soup.

In large soup pot, place 6 cups broth, 1 1/2 lbs peeled, sliced carrots, 1 1/2 lbs sliced sweet potatoes or yams, 1 T minced ginger root, 1/2 chopped onion, 2 peeled, cored, chopped apples, 1/3 cup oats (use old fashioned if possible), and 1 T curry powder. Bring to a boil, reduce heat and cover. Simmer 25 minutes until the vegetables are soft. Use a potato masher to crush vegetables to a soupy consistency, add salt and pepper to taste and a sprinkling of parsley or coriander and enjoy! As a variation, this is delicious served over steamed rice. Omit the mashing if served this way. Serves 4.

Lentil Rice Pilaf

We like to rustle up this hearty and delicious dish on winter cruises. Its tasty blend of flavors will satisfy all appetites. Serve as a whole meal vegetarian dish, or with grilled chicken or fish as an accompaniment.

Saute 1/2 chopped onion in 2 T olive oil until soft. Add 1 cup raw brown rice (ok to substitute whatever white rice you have on hand), and cook, stirring for several minutes; add 2 T tomato paste and 1/2 t cinnamon. Next, add 1/2 cup raw lentils. Bring to a boil, cover tightly, reduce heat to very low, and simmer for 30 minutes. Stir in 1 t salt, 1/2 c sunflower seeds, 2 cloves minced garlic, 2 T parsley and 1/2 cup golden raisins. Coat a 9x13 baking dish with 1 T oil and pour in rice mixture. Cover and bake at 350 degrees for 25 minutes. Serves 4

High Seas Mueseli Bread

Is there anything better than munching on a slice of home-made bread? This bread, dense and rich with flavor, is a great breakfast and snack energizer. It is well worth the trouble to make sure you've packed along the more unusual ingredients. Begin this the night before:

Mix together 2/3 cup sunflower seeds, 1/3 cup flax seeds (or 1/3 cup sesame seeds), 1 cup rolled oats and 1 1/2 cup rye meal (or rye flour). Stir in 1 1/2 cups warm water and let sit overnight.

In another bowl, mix 2 cups white flour, 1 cup warm water and 1/2 T yeast. Cover tightly and refrigerate overnight.

The next day, combine the seed mixture with the yeast mixture. To this, add 2 cups white flour, 1 1/2 cups rye flour or meal, 1 t salt, 1/3 cup honey, 1/4 cup corn oil and 1/2 T yeast. Knead for 8 minutes. Add in 1/2 cup chopped pecans, 1/2 cup chopped almonds and 1 cup dried cranberries.

Let dough rest for 30 minutes. Divide and shape into 2 loaves. Place on greased baking sheet and let rise 1 hour, or until doubled.

Place a pan of hot water on lowest shelf of a pre-heated 425 degree oven, bake loaves for 10 minutes, reduce heat to 400 degrees and continue baking for another 40 minutes more.

Wild Greens Side Kick

Sometimes it is very pleasant to take a walk with a purpose: identify the plants you see ashore, find out what is edible and convert this basic wild greens dish to what you can find. (Janice Schofield's wonderful book, *Discovering Wild Plants*, is a great resource for recipes and plant identification.) This also works equally well with store bought chard, spinach, beet greens and other dark winter greens.

Saute 1 chopped onion and 1 t minced ginger root in 1 T oil until tender. Stir in 1 1/2 cups washed wild greens such as nettles, dandelion, chickweed, lamb's quarter, and lovage leaves. Add 1 T soy sauce and 1 T Dijon mustard. Cover and cook over low heat for a few minutes until wilted. Serves 2-3 as a side dish

Garbanzo Salad

We love the zesty taste of this summer supper salad. Don't be reluctant to add the garlic: we have found that the mosquitoes are less enamored of us after we eat it.

For dressing, mix and let stand: 2 cloves minced garlic, 2 T dried mint, 3 T olive oil, 3 T lemon juice (or vinegar), 1/2 t each salt and pepper.

Into a large bowl put 8 ounces pimento, two 15 oz. cans garbanzos, rinsed and drained, 4 T dried chives, 1 T celery flakes and 2 T capers. Pour dressing over this, cover and serve within 24 hours. Serves 4

Note: 2 chopped red sweet peppers, 1/2 cup sliced green onions, 1/2 cup chopped celery and 3 T fresh mint may be used in place of their dried counterparts, if desired (and possible).

Pasta Salad

The liquid from the hearts of palm make a light, tasty dressing. Almost any kind of short pasta works in this quick and good dish.

Cook 1 handful of pasta per person. Rinse and drain well. Put in a large bowl with 6 oz. drained marinated artichoke hearts, 7 oz. hearts of palm, 15 oz. can drained cut tomatoes, 6 oz. sliced canned mushrooms, or a handful of dried Shitake mushrooms rehydrated in boiling water then sliced, 1 cup sliced black olives, 2 T dried chives, 1 T parsley, 1 t basil and salt and pepper to taste. Cover and refrigerate for at least 4 hours. Serves 6.

Dunkers

Don't panic if you have run out of sweet treats for tea time! These remarkably good cookies require no butter or eggs, and with the addition of jam on top look very festive for a special occasion. They have a satisfactory crunch that makes dunking them into the tea almost irresistible!

Sift together 2 1/2 cups flour, 1 1/2 t baking powder, 3/4 t salt, 1 t cinnamon, 1/4 t nutmeg and 1/4 t ginger.

Mix 1 cup sugar and 3/4 cup vegetable oil; combine with flour mixture. Now add 3 t egg replacer, 4 T water and 1 t vanilla and beat well. Shape dough into 1" balls, flatten and score in a decorative manner with a fork or spoon. Bake at 375 degrees 10 to 12 minutes on a greased cookie sheet. Makes about 4 dozen.

Berry Roll

The recollection of summer berries, sweet and warm, hanging from laden bushes, rambling along a sunny hillside ready for the picking is almost enough to see us through the bad parts of winter. This recipe is best with 5 cups of fresh berries in any combination. Blackberries, raspberries, huckleberries, salmon berries, blueberries, thimble berries and whatever else is in your area will create a gorgeous base for this dessert. Canned berries may be used in a pinch, but adjust for the extra sugar from the canned syrup.

First, mix 1 cup sugar with 1 3/4 cups water and simmer on low heat 5 minutes. Pour this into a greased 9 x13 baking pan and let cool to room temperature. Next mix a soft Bisquick dough with 2 1/4 cups Bisquick and 2/3 cup canned milk. Gently roll the dough out to a 12 x 8 rectangle. Spread 2 cups berries over this and sprinkle with 4 T sugar and 1/2 t cinnamon. Roll the dough and berries up, pinching shut at seams. Cut the roll into 1" wide slices, arrange in the 9 x 13 pan in the syrup, put remaining 3 cups of berries over the slices, pushing them down into the syrup. Bake at 450 degrees for 25 minutes. Makes 8 - 16 servings.

Dried Fruit Compote

Dried fruit is an easy item to pack and makes a nice nonperishable contribution to the galley stores. It also provides a good little munching item, which seems to be in demand quite a lot on boats. This is an elegant, rich dessert.

Bring 2 cups apple juice, 1 cup each dried apricots, figs and cranberries, and a cinnamon stick to boil. Reduce heat and cover and cook 15 minutes, stirring occasionally. Uncover and cook until all liquid evaporates, stirring frequently. Cool completely, remove cinnamon stick. Add 1/2 cup chopped pecans. Dish a small amount out for each serving with a little sherry and canned milk drizzled on the top. Serves 6

Stars

Delightful as the promise of a warm bunk and a good book are, you will miss a great chance to stargaze if you turn in too early. The sky seems infinitely deeper and darker when you are out on the water and, with fewer city lights to compete, an extravagant celestial show may be yours. It makes sense to know a few things about the stars; it could come in handy in case the electronics give out!

With some knowledge of the stars, you will be able to determine roughly where you are and in what general direction you are headed. (This sounds a bit like knowing that moss grows on the north side of trees. O.K., so you know you are at x latitude and are in the Northern Hemisphere...but where exactly is the harbor? Keep in mind that sailors did a lot of impressive navigating with very little except the stars back in the old days.) Actually, learning about the stars is a good excuse to stay up and enjoy a romantic evening sky.

Learning and identifying the stars and constellations may seem overwhelming, but it's not. Out of 88 constellations only about 60 can be seen in our northern latitudes and only 24 are visible at a time. If you learn the most interesting stars and half the constellations, you'll have a pretty good working knowledge of the sky.

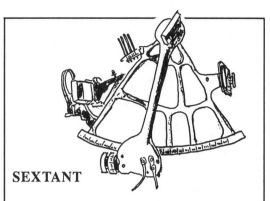

SEXTANT

The sextant is used for offshore navigating where the only aids are in the sky. By measuring the angle between the horizon and some celestial body at a known time, it is possible to determine your line of position (LOP). This principle was discovered in 1730 by Thomas Godfrey of Philadelphia and John Hadley of London. The graduated metal strip, shaped in an arc of the sixth part of a circle, gave the instrument its name.

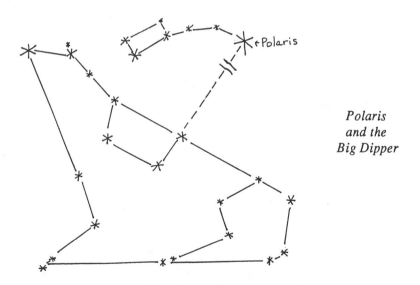

*Polaris
and the
Big Dipper*

The most important star is POLARIS, so named because it is at the north pole of the sky and the entire sky appears to be moving around it. Polaris is also known as the NORTH STAR because it is almost exactly north. If you face Polaris, you face north; east is on your right, west to your left and south to your back. You can locate Polaris by extending the cup edge of the Big Dipper farthest away from the handle about five times out.

For the stars in the sky, one turn around Polaris takes 23 hours and 56 minutes. That four minute gap in our 24 hour clock means that the stars rise four minutes earlier every day than the day before. This all adds up! Some stars are best seen in spring, some in winter, some in fall and some in the summer sky. The sky appears to rotate, but the stars never change their positions relative to each other. The constellations rise (or seem to) in the east and set in the west once a day. We focus here on the brightest and most interesting stars and constellations which can be seen in the northern latitudes: the Big Dipper, Little Dipper, Ursa Major (Great Bear), Cassiopeia, the Twins (Gemini), Charioteer (Auriga) and Orion.

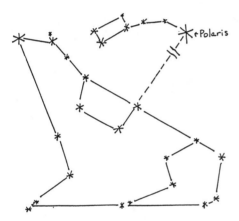

BIG DIPPER is actually a group of stars, not a constellation by itself. Its parent constellation, URSA MAJOR, is one of the 88 officially recognized constellations. It helps us find POLARIS, which is also the tip of the handle of the LITTLE DIPPER (URSA MINOR). The Big and Little Dippers can be seen year round.

Ursa Major

CASSIOPEIA, easy to spot by its clear 'W' shape, is formed by five stars. It can be seen August through January.

Cassiopia

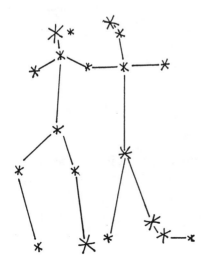

The TWINS (GEMINI), may be seen on a clear night December through May. The two heads are Castor and Pollux, the bodies are more faint.

Gemini twins

The CHARIOTEER (AURIGA), is shaped like a face under a pointed cap. The bright eye is CAPELLA, an enormous, brilliant and always present star which is also the name of the Bradfield family boat. This star can be located by going across the lip of the Big Dipper's cup and out.

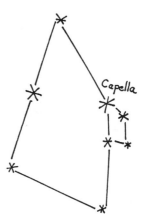

Auriga

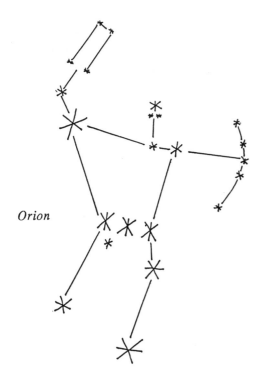

Orion

ORION is an impressive constellation best seen December through March. Locate Orion by finding the three bright stars of his belt and tracing the figure from there. You will see a hunter with a raised club, a sword dangling, and a shield at arm's length. Two additional bright stars are Betelgeuse (left shoulder) and Rigel (right foot).

Twinkle, twinkle
Little star.
How I wonder
What you are!

The planets, which do not twinkle, appear to wander around among the constellations. Five planets can be seen with the naked eye: Mercury, Venus, Mars, Jupiter and Saturn.

Venus, the brightest and easiest to spot, can be found above the western horizon after sunset (the Evening Star) or above the eastern horizon (the Morning Star). Jupiter is quite bright and can be seen high, low, east, west, or south at any time of the night as can Mars and Saturn. Mars' brilliance varies, but always has a reddish cast.

Remember that the planets give a steady light.

At the Wheel
Figuring Out What Is Going On

Charts

Charts are inexpensive and often beautiful. Along with the compass, they are the Captain's most important navigating tool. Consider buying your own chart or charts to mark for a great souvenir of your trip. It's nice to have a record on your own chart of the highlights and a way of finding the special places again. Note catching the giant fish, the best crab, eating at the perfect picnic spot, skinny-dipping at the hidden swimming hole, or finding a patch of wild blackberries. Use your own system to mark events and locations and also, better yet, learn how to properly read the chart for navigating.

Detail of nautical chart

Chart basics

Reading a chart is more complicated than following a road map. There is a lot of information to help you and much of it has to do with the movement of the water.

Why is there so much movement? In most areas the water is greatly affected by tides and currents. Tides are a vertical measurement; they go up and down. Currents, on the other hand, are the horizontal movement of the water at either ebb, slack or flood.

Tides occur in oceans and seas. Their effect may also be noticeable many miles up a coastal river. They range from almost nothing to fifty feet in different parts of the world.

U.S. charts, published by three different agencies of the Federal Government, are created from extensive research and continuous updating to give important navigational information. The three areas are the high seas and foreign waters (DMAHTC), coastal waters and tidal rivers (NOAA), and lakes, canal systems and some rivers (Army Corps of Engineers). Canadian waters are charted by Canada's Department of Fisheries and Oceans.

Terms having to do with tides

EBB = water flowing toward the sea (falling tide).
FLOOD = water flowing toward the land (rising tide).
SLACK = water movement basically stopped when the time of high water or low water approaches. Slack is what you have to wait for to maneuver certain channels. For example, if you must travel through a channel when the current against you reaches 8 knots and your speed is only 6 knots, you will be going backward!

Currents can be present in coastal waters, bays, rivers, seas, oceans and lakes — in short, where there is water. An area may have little or no tide, but be affected by a tricky current from strong breezes.

It is important to observe the movement of water around buoys or other objects in the water to get an idea of the current's strength, speed and direction.

Reading the chart

1. Find out if the chart is using fathoms, meters or feet so you will know the depth of the water.

2. Determine whether the chart is small scale (covering a big area), or large scale (covering a small area).

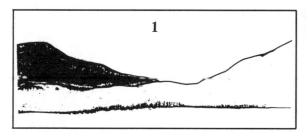

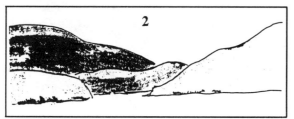

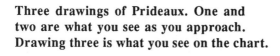

Three drawings of Prideaux. One and two are what you see as you approach. Drawing three is what you see on the chart.

3. Locate the lines of latitude and longitude. Latitude runs east-west, parallel to the Equator, with zero degrees at the Equator and a maximum of 90 degrees at the poles. Longitude runs north-south through the poles and will give your position as x degrees east or west of 0, the Prime Meridian (Greenwich, England).

4. Locate the numbers indicating depth of water. (See the chart above.)

The numbers are all over the blue and white (water) areas of the chart, giving you some idea of the contours of the sea (or lake or river) floor. These numbers are the average shallow depth of the water in those particular areas based on the Mean Lower Low Water. Huh? The MLLW is the average of the lowest tides of the year.

5. Note the chart's different color codes:

- White = open sea, deep, safe water
- Blue = shallow
- Green = bare land at low tide, covered at high tide
- Tan = dry land above Mean High Water
- Purple marks = lighthouses and buoys

6. Understand the abbreviations:

Cl = clay	**Hrd** = hard
Rk = rock	**Rky** = rocky
Grs = grass	**M** = mud
S = sand	**Sft** = soft

7. Other symbols to note:

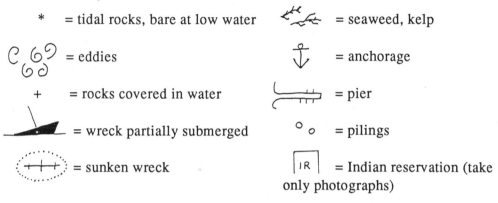

*   = tidal rocks, bare at low water   = seaweed, kelp

= eddies   = anchorage

+   = rocks covered in water   = pier

= wreck partially submerged   = pilings

= sunken wreck   = Indian reservation (take only photographs)

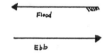

tiny arrows = with feathers, the arrows indicate the direction of the current at flood; without feathers they indicate direction at ebb.

We've listed only some basic symbols and abbreviations. If you want to know more, your Captain probably has *Chart No. 1 United States of America Nautical Chart Symbols and Abbreviations*. This is a government book that explains all the symbols used on charts.

On a beautiful evening after sunset, Barbara and Guest went for a row. The night was clear, calm and warm. Although it was nine o'clock, the evening light was still bright and flat darkness seemed a long way off. They hightailed it away to avoid dish duty, figuring to return in time for dessert. With the idea of exploring their lagoon and a bit beyond, they proceeded on a pleasant, meandering course watching the sea-life and beautiful reflections in the water. They decided to circumnavigate the little island on their right, which would eventually bring them back to the *Capella*. Having set this goal, they took turns rowing and made pretty good progress. It was much darker now, as it is away from civilization on a moonless night, and the only distinction between shore and water was a denser blackness at the water's edge. They began rowing in earnest and could feel a significant tug of the current pulling

them back. This was still fun exercise, but how big was this island, anyway? At 11:30 p.m., they heard a humming sound (a big generator) and saw a series of lights. The little settlement at the front of the lagoon! No sooner had they spotted the lights and began to row toward them, the big generator quit for the night and the lights went off. Almost at that same moment, the light from the *Capella's* bow made a quick sweep over them a couple of times, and they knew dessert was about fifteen minutes away. Little did they realize that all aboard the mother ship were worried and had sent off part of the crew to try to find them. The spotlight had not identified them and the crew assumed that they had been swept off in the current, injured or lost. Later when all were back on board, Barbara and Guest did a postmortem of their adventure. They should have checked the chart before setting off to orient themselves; if they had done so they would have realized that the island's circumference was a distance of four miles — too far for a spur-of-the-moment row. They should have taken a flashlight and a small hand-held radio. They should have given the Captain some idea of where they were headed and how long they would be gone. Barbara and Guest loved the row. Too bad they blew it by needlessly worrying the crew.

Buoys and beacons in North America
(Pronounced 'boo-ie' on the West Coast, 'boy' in the East.)

Important aids to navigation shown on the chart are buoys and beacons. Buoys float, while beacons are fixed on land. This is important to remember because buoys are affected by the movement of the water and may be located a bit farther afield than what you'd expected from seeing them on the chart. Buoys and beacons warn you of danger and mark significant hazards and channels.

Buoys have different shapes, colors, lights and sounds to show their purpose. They are red (R), green (G), red and white (RW), red and green (RG or GR) and black and white (BW). The U.S. buoyage system is known as the Lateral System, which was devised to show on which side boats should pass.

Unlighted RED buoys in the water are called NUNS (N), cone shaped with even numbers (2,4,6 etc.).

A NUN in the water: On the chart, they are shown as a magenta diamond.

NUNS' numbers increase as you go into port or farther upstream. These buoys are to be kept on your starboard side when you are technically returning from the sea (RED RIGHT RETURNING). Generally, the buoyage system follows the U.S. coast in a clockwise direction down the Atlantic Coast, west across the Gulf of Mexico and north along the Pacific Coast toward Alaska.

In the Great Lakes, the system is different. Red buoys mark the starboard side when sailing west or north, except in Lake Michigan where south is considered to be the returning-from-the sea direction.

Because buoys float at the end of an anchor rode, they may not be in precisely the location indicated on the chart. For this reason, give a sensibly wide berth to buoys to avoid hitting whatever hazard it is they mark. When you look at the chart you can usually see that the buoy symbol indicates good advice. Keep looking at the chart and the water to track where you are.

Unlighted GREEN buoys in the water are called CANS (C), flat topped and cylindrical with odd numbers (1,3,5 etc.).

A CAN in the water. These are shown on the chart by a green diamond (right)

(Canadian charts show starboard buoys in magenta and port buoys in black, though the port buoys are green in the water.) See the magenta discs scattered around on the chart with red or green diamonds coming out of them? These symbols represent lighted buoys. The numbers by these discs on the chart indicate the flashing patterns of the light that will help you pick out the buoys at night (e.g. Fl R 3s means a red light that flashes on every three seconds). When you sight them in the water, green buoys will have a green light and red buoys will have a red light.

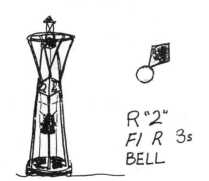

A larger, lighted buoy in the water. On the chart, they look like the illustration on the right.

MID-CHANNEL buoys are vertically striped (red and white) and spherical in shape, are not numbered but may be lettered. On the chart they are unshaded diamonds with a vertical line.

When lighted they have a white light flashing the Morse Code letter "A" (a short then a long flash). The lighted mid-channel buoy is also shown on the chart by an unshaded diamond with a vertical line and, additionally, a small circle at both the top and bottom and the letters RW and MoA. Vessels should pass a mid-channel buoy close on either side.

DAYMARKERS are found in shallow water, are not lighted and are permanently fixed, often on pilings.

A lighted mid-channel buoy in the water. On the chart you see this symbol on the right

From the boat you see red triangles with even numbers and triangle daymarkers on the right (RED RIGHT RETURNING) and green squares with odd numbers on the left. Remember this easily: triangles have three points and the word red has three letters.

Daymarks with chart symbols

When entering a harbor, you will also see PREFERRED CHANNEL DAYMARKERS, which are colored red and green. The square markers with green on top and red on the bottom tell you the principal channel is to starboard.

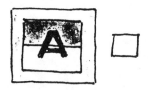

Preferred channel daymarker with chart symbol

The red triangles with the top red and the bottom green indicate the principal channel is to port.

Triangular preferred channel daymarker

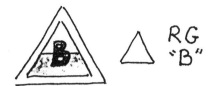

NUNS and CANS can also indicate the preferred channel by the color of the uppermost band (either red or green). They are seen in the water and on the chart:

NUN and chart symbol   *CAN and chart symbol*

Ranges are also an important navigational aid. They are helpful beacons in tricky situations and come in a variety of colors and shapes, some lighted some not, some lettered and some numbered. These fixed beacons are

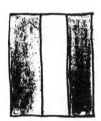

often present in rivers, harbors and channels. The idea is to line up two ranges vertically, which tells you that you are in the channel and on the range. Care must be taken to keep on the range, not miss the turning point, and not be swept aside by wind or current.

Guests can help by watching with the Captain as the boat travels between the front and rear ranges. On the chart, ranges are indicated by a solid line and a dashed line between two points. The solid line is intended for navigation and the dashed line is not navigable. Care is taken to stay on the solid line segment, which means safe water.

Square vertical ranges

The magenta exclamation points on the chart are symbols for fixed, lighted beacons on land that are used as reference points or mark dangerous areas. Note that the written information given for these is the same as for lighted buoys (Fl G 4s).

Many of these beacons are lighthouses, indicated as LtHo on the chart. At this time in the United States, the single remaining manned lighthouse is in Boston. All other lights are controlled by automation. Canada still has manned lighthouses and we hope they will continue to be tended by lighthouse keepers. It is reassuring to know that an actual person is there in the tower, assisting with safety, communication and sometimes ready to visit.

You will also see symbols for light characteristics. What do the LIGHT characteristic symbols on the chart mean?

oc = occulting; duration of light is longer than dark. This is pretty unusual and will be found only in a busy harbor such as San Francisco Bay.

Fl = flashing; duration of light less than the darker periods. Most lights on a chart will be Fl.

E int = equal interval of light and dark periods (Isophase)

m or ft = height of light is in meters or feet. You need to know this to figure out your distance from the beacon.

M = range of light in miles

There are a few more light symbols. Your Captain will have additional information.

Cape Hatteras lighthouse

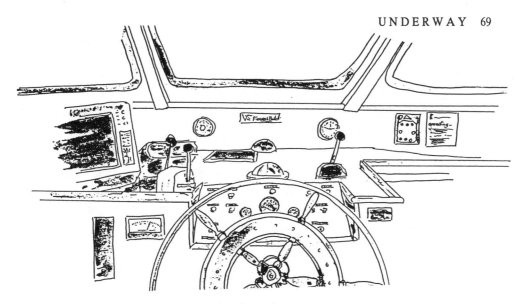

At the wheel

It is now time to come to terms with the nitty-gritty of being a helpful, capable crew member. Time to step up there and take the wheel! Before you do this, a basic understanding of the compass is necessary.

The COMPASS is an essential navigational tool, simple to use if you get the reading of it straight in your head. First, ask the Captain if the boat's compass is a gyro or magnetic. The gyro compass headings read True North and the magnetic compass headings read Magnetic North. Gyros are usually on the great big fancy yachts and tour boats. We'll only discuss using the magnetic compass here because it's likely that if you have the chance to steer, you are on a smaller boat and your compass will be magnetic.

The Marine compass is a circular card divided into 360 degrees. North is either 0 degrees or 360 degrees, east is 90 degrees, south is 180 degrees and west is 270 degrees. The N on the card always points to Magnetic North on magnetic compasses. This card is on a pivot pin set in oil in a bowl and on the far side of the bowl is a mark, the Lubber's Line. To steer a particular compass heading (say, 176 degrees), you align the lubber line with the course heading on the disc.

The compass number at the lubber line is your bow direction. The compass may be affected by metal objects on the boat. Your Captain will have checked the compass for this deviation, the difference between the compass reading and the magnetic heading. Find out what this number is so that you can accurately plot a course.

Practicing steering

It is important to practice steering to see what turning the boat does to the compass heading. During a relatively quiet passage, ask permission to try your hand at the wheel or tiller.

> The term "lubber line" comes from inexperienced sailors' (land lubbers') dependence on this guide for steering rather than using the stars and other objects used by experienced seamen.

Does a quarter turn of the wheel turn the boat 10, 20, 30 degrees? How quickly does the boat respond to major and minor heading corrections?   Handling a boat is very different from steering a car; in a car with four tires stuck to the road you need only be aware of what is happening beside, in front of and behind you. Driving a boat, on the other hand, is more like flying an airplane where the environment is three-dimensional. The boating traffic must be dealt with as well as the effects of the weather (above) and the currents (below). You are moving through the water, rather than on it, and the various forces affecting your movement must be reckoned with, for they frequently provide surprises. Your Captain will appreciate your understanding this.

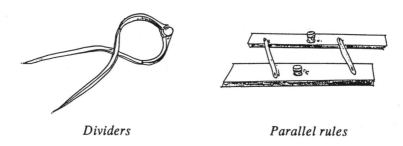

Dividers   *Parallel rules*

Plotting a course

The tools needed to plot a course are a chart, dividers for measuring distance, a straight-edged tool such as parallel rules, and a parallel plotter or two triangles. If you are working with the ship's charts, be careful not to mark the Captain's charts in any way without permission.

Now see the Compass Rose on the chart. Usually the Compass Rose has two circles. The two circles represent True North (outside circle) and Magnetic North (inside circle). Most boats use a magnetic compass, so the Rose's inner circle is used. (You have already asked your Captain about the

boat's compass type, right?)
The difference between the
inner circle reading
(magnetic) and the outer
circle (true north) reading is
the VARIATION. (This
variation is caused by the
difference in location
between the geographical
north pole and the magnetic
north pole.) The variation is
on every chart and is seen
on the Compass Rose in the
center.

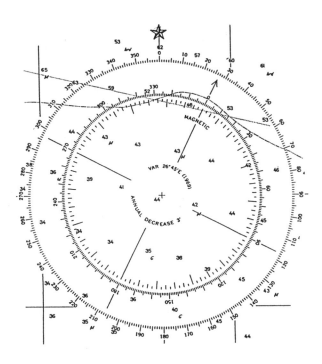

Compass rose

With a series of straight
lines you lay down a path
toward your destination.
Use a pencil and straight
edge to mark this course.
This is the course you want
to follow. Keep in mind that
your course must be far enough away from the land to avoid shallow
waters and obstacles, but aiming as directly as possible toward your
destination. Read the chart with care. See the symbols and correctly
interpret them.

Next, carefully walk the parallel rules or roll the parallel plotter from the
course line to the middle of the Rose. Be as accurate as possible and avoid
slippage. Always use the heading on the magnetic (inner) circle. Think
about which way you are going or your numbers may be exactly 180
degrees off. There is a big, embarrassing difference between 42 degrees
and 222 degrees!

The compass heading is written on top of the course line. This course is
called a magnetic course and is labeled with the letter M (124M, for
example). This magnetic course could be further modified by taking into
account deviation (the boat's compass error caused by electronics or metal
objects near the compass), winds and / or currents if significant.

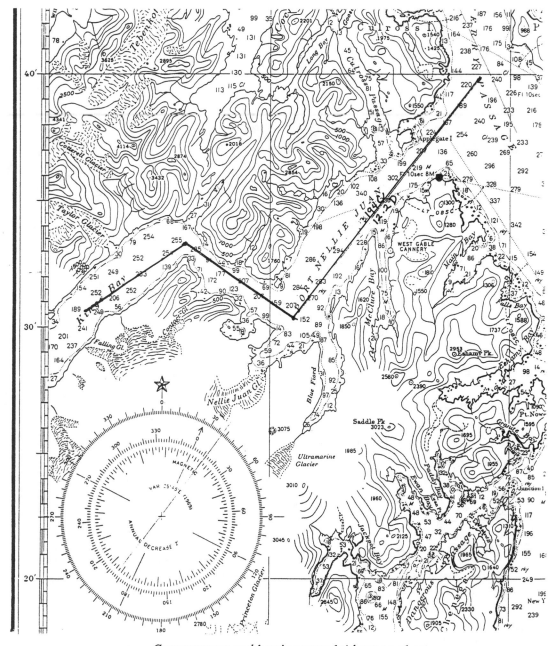

Compass rose and boat's course laid out on chart

Next, use the dividers to figure out the distance to be traveled. Separate the points and move them to the latitude scale on the left or right margin of the chart (never the longitude at the top or bottom). One minute of latitude equals one nautical mile, or 6076.1 feet. On land we use the statute mile, which is 5280 feet. The statute mile is also used on rivers. After you calculate the distance (D), it is customary to put this information under the compass heading, below the course line. Have someone check your calculations for accuracy.

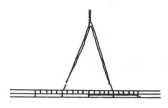

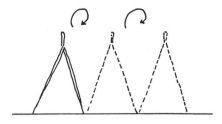

Dividers   *Using dividers to measure distance*

Are you wondering if you should bother to do any of this? Give it a try. It is fun to know where you are, to see where you are headed and how long it will take to get there. Be the official boat psychic and fill in the formula 60D=ST (60 x distance equals speed x time in minutes). Astound your hosts and friends with your powers of predicting the ETA's!

Rules of the Road

Now that you have some knowledge of navigating, your next big responsibility is to understand and use the Rules of the Road. The Rules, also known as COLREGS, from *The International Regulations for Preventing Collision at Sea*, were created to govern the rights of way between boats. If followed, the Rules reduce confusion, create harmony afloat and, most importantly, prevent collisions. The COLREGS apply to all vessels at all times except when local regulations override those rules or when common sense and good seamanship dictate another choice:

"The responsibility for the vessel remains with the skipper at all times, and if the safety of his ship requires him to depart from the rules, then depart he must."

At the helm, it is your obligation to watch carefully and anticipate what may happen in the waters around you. Travel at a speed safe enough to allow you to stop, slow down or take evasive maneuvers in time to prevent

Boat at anchor in peaceful bay

a collision. The dangerous aspect of boating has much to do with ignorance of Rules of the Road. It is comforting to assume that everyone is equally well educated, but don't. When you are out there, at the wheel with a crossing situation coming up, you have no way of knowing that the other boat will behave as it should. Be alert and observant. If in doubt, ask the Captain.

At the Helm

Most accidents occur because of the operator's lack of attention. If you are the helmsperson, it is important to be attentive to these details:

- Keep a proper lookout at all times while underway.
- Be sure to attend to blind areas caused by sails or deckhouses.
- Look behind you to check for traffic off the stern.
- Determine the risk of collision: align the other boat with a stanchion or mast and see how she moves relative to the stanchion. If she stays in line with the stanchion, you will collide. If she moves forward of the stanchion, she will cross your bow. If she moves aft of the stanchion, she will pass astern. It takes practice to be good at making this judgement call, so try predicting when someone else is at the helm to polish your skill.
- Listen carefully in the fog. You will also be sounding your horn every two minutes.
- Use running lights from sunset to sunrise and in poor visibility.

Simple Rules

Remembering that port is red ("Sailors drink red port.") and starboard is green, follow these simple rules:

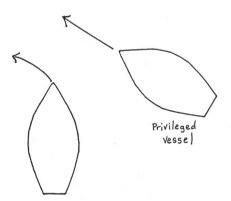

Privileged
Vessel

If you see green (the other boat's starboard side), you have the right of way and are the PRIVILEGED VESSEL. It is your duty to maintain your course and speed and allow the other boat to give way. Alter your course and speed only to avoid a collision.

At times you needn't change course at all:

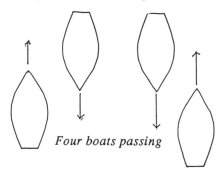

Four boats passing

Green to Green
or Red to Red
Perfect safety
Go ahead.

If you approach another boat head-on, you will usually alter your course to starboard and pass port to port.

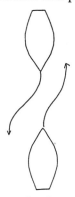

*Boat altering course to
starboard*

*If RED and GREEN
you see ahead,
starboard wheel
and show your red.*

Turn to the right as if you were on a road.

If it makes more sense to pass starboard to starboard, make your move early and stick to it.

When must you change course for the other guy?
If you come upon the other boat's port side, you are the GIVE-WAY, vessel. (The older term 'BURDENED' is being phased out.) Decide what to do, take action early enough so the other boat doesn't panic, and make your course change obvious enough to be clearly seen.

*If to starboard RED appears,
it is your duty to stand clear."*

If you are overtaking another boat, you must keep clear of that boat's path. It is best to pass to starboard under the other boat's stern.

Overtaking: passing to starboard

Sailboats and Rules of the Road

The rules are somewhat different for powerboats and sailboats. When two boats are sailing, the rules are:

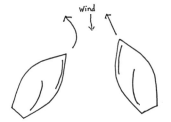

Sailboat with wind on port turns away

- When each has the wind on a different side, the vessel with the wind on her port side must keep out of the way of the other.

- When both have the wind on the same side, the vessel that is windward must keep out of the way of the boat to leeward (the one farthest from the wind).

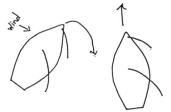

Two boats, wind on same side: windward boat turns away

If to port or if in doubt
Or if to windward get on out.

- Sailboats, if under sail, have the right of way over powerboats. However, if the sailboat is overtaking the powerboat, or if the powerboat is too large to easily maneuver (like a tanker), the sailboat should yield the right of way.

Powerboats and Rules of the Road

It is not courteous for powerboats to cross the bow of a sailing sailboat nor to pass too closely to windward.

All powerboats must:

- keep out of the way of vessels unable to maneuver or not under command, and vessels fishing

- give ferries and large commercial vessels right of way because of their slow maneuverability.

Power and Sail

Be sure to look around carefully before changing your course. Check your stern, port and starboard areas. Leave enough time and space to ensure a comfort zone for all.

Rules of the Road can be confusing. It takes a long time and lots of different episodes to feel confident at the wheel. Be calm and remember to call the Captain if you feel unsure.

> **Recite this piece of advice to yourself and others as needed:**
>
> **Here lies the body of Jonathan Day Who died maintaining his right of way.**
> **He was right, dead right. He was right all along,**
> **But he's just as dead as if he was wrong.**

Whistles

short blast (.) = one second
long blast (-) = four to six seconds

You will hear whistles and horns while out cruising or at anchor. They are used to clarify confusing passing situations and to signal locations in the fog. As a guest you will probably not have to use whistles while navigating, but it is nice to know what that noise means. Keep this list handy:

- **One short blast** (.) = Passing port to port
- **Two short blasts** (..) = Passing starboard to starboard
- **Two long blasts** (--) = I intend to overtake you
- **Three short blasts** (...) = Engine is in reverse
- **One long blast** (-) every two minutes = Am in fog and underway
- **Two long blasts** (--) every two minutes = Am stopped
- **Four or more short blasts** (....) = Danger / Doubt
- **Three short** (...) **three long** (---) **three short** (...) = SOS

In international waters, only a signal of the action taken is given. An answering signal is never given.

You'll be passing the Banks of Newfoundland, a most picturesque experience. In thick weather (which is practically constant) you'll be aware of a curious hollow noise. That will be the barking of the Newfoundland dogs who are trained to sit on the Banks and warn ships of the treacherous shoals.
— Our Hearts Were Young and Gay,
Cornelia Otis Skinner and Emily Kimborough

Flags

It is a wonderful sight to see boats with several flags snapping in the breeze. The festive air this creates is appreciated, but the main purpose of the flags is to identify the boat. You will notice that boats usually have three identifying flags: the ensign, the burgee and the house flag.

Maccoboy with flags

The ENSIGN, usually flown from the stern on powerboats and the afterpeak or the stern on sailboats, shows her country of origin. It is flown from sunrise to sunset.

The triangular BURGEE, flown at the bow on powerboats or the foremost masthead on sailboats, indicates fleet or organization affiliation, such as a yacht club.

The Master's private HOUSE FLAG, flown from the signal masthead on powerboats or starboard spreader on sailboats, is strictly personal and usually simple and symbolic to the owner.

As a friendly gesture in foreign waters, vessels may fly the host country's flag. This COURTESY FLAG is flown on the starboard side shroud or the spreader or on the bow staff. The flag is taken down when the boat leaves the foreign waters.

Before VHF radio, flags were used to communicate with other vessels. Some boats still carry a set of International Code flags.

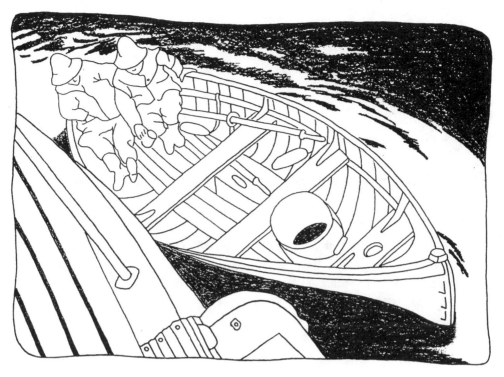

5
NOT UNDERWAY

Captain! My Captain! our fearful trip is done
— **Walt Whitman**

At the end of the day's cruising, your Captain will find a safe harbor to "drop the hook," or tie up to a dock or a mooring buoy.

Anchoring

Anchoring the boat is an interesting and challenging process. As a guest, you will want to have a general idea about what to expect and to think about ways you might assist.

First, at the Captain's signal, tend the dinghy line by shortening it up toward the boat. If you are in a power boat, wait until the engine is out of gear before attempting to pull the dinghy up. The Captain will approach the anchorage slowly and stop at the point where the anchor will rest on the bottom. Notice that your boat is anchored far enough away from the other boats so that there is plenty of swinging room. Look at the way the other boats are riding at their anchors and expect that your position after anchoring will be one to three times farther astern at the same heading as the other bows.

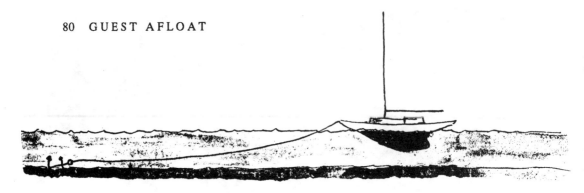

Rode ratio with boat anchored

With the boat stopped, the anchor is let down. You will drift on back slowly, or use minimal power to put a gradual strain on the anchor rope or chain to help set the anchor. The anchor line is probably marked with paint or tabs; pay attention to these markings because they help you keep track of how much line is let out. If chain is used, the scope should be a ratio of 3 to 1. This means that the length of the chain (rode) will be three times as long as the water is deep.

If rope is used, and depending on the type of anchor, the scope should be at least 5 to 1. If the wind comes up you will let out more line and increase the ratio to 7 to 1. (Note: We realize that the United States Power Squadrons' manual recommends a greater ratio than 3 to 1 and 5 to 1. In our experience, many harbors are too crowded to allow for the longer scope and swinging range of the boats.) Check to see that the anchor is holding fast by lining up landmarks on the shore. The Captain will have carefully calculated tide changes to ensure that there will be enough scope. The boat's anchor light remains on during the night.

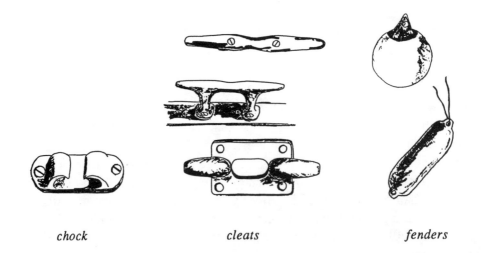

chock   *cleats*   *fenders*

Docking

Before docking, shorten the dinghy line to prevent it from fouling (tangling up) the propellers, help hang fenders, and place lines according to the Captain's direction. Be prepared to switch all fenders and lines to the opposite side at the last minute. This usually creates groans and consternation in the crew, but the Captain sometimes cannot be certain which side will be tied to the dock until the boat is almost there and so must make a last-minute decision.

Docking is done quietly.
There is no yelling.

It helps to have prearranged signals between Captain and crew. A whistle is often used to communicate: two short blasts means "Go astern," one short blast means "Go forward."

Some prefer hand signals: the classic "Halt" gesture means stop, a beckoning hand means "Come forward." No doubt the Captain and Mate will have already determined what works best for them. The practicality of these signals depends on the size of the boat, the visibility afforded the Captain, and how much the Captain trusts the signaler's judgement in giving directions.

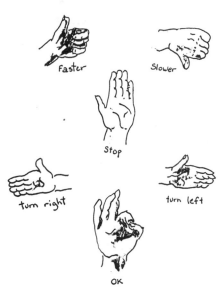

Hand signals

As the Captain pulls gently alongside the dock, the action begins. It is crucial that you understand which line is to be secured (tied firmly) first: bow, stern, or mid-ship. All line handlers need to know this in advance. The Captain depends on working that line to position the boat to the dock.

If you think this is your moment for trying out that Olympic jump to the dock, forget it. Plan to step off carefully to avoid swimming unexpectedly or wedging a leg between boat and dock. The dock lines should all be neatly coiled in hand and ready to either be thrown to someone on the dock or taken to the dock by you.

**NEVER try to save a poor docking by putting your arm
or leg between the boat and the dock!
FEND OFF WITH FENDERS!**

A word about the folks on the dock — these are often over-eager, but inexperienced landlubbers anxious to help get your boat tied up. Unless you are coming in to a gas dock or a marina where T-shirts identify paid help, you have no way of knowing how useful anyone on the docks' assistance will be. Some folks long to get their hands on your lines and pull you on in, never mind what the Captain's intention is. Find out how to deal with this situation before it happens. Ask the Captain and Mate for directions on how to tactfully decline or direct the help you are offered.

Shore picnic

Ashore

When you have finished traveling and are tied up at the dock or anchored out, it's fun to go off to explore the area. The Good Guest will see this as a chance to give other people on board space and time alone. Before leaving, take a look at the chart to orient yourself and see if there are any interesting coves or lagoons for dinghy sight-seeing.

Dinghies deserve a special checklist:

1. adequate life jackets (one per person)
2. paddle or oars in case the engine quits
3. sufficient fuel
4. bailer
5. whistle or noisemaker (the Coast Guard requires this)
6. flashlight at night
7. chart and a few navigational tools such as a compass if the journey warrants
8. line to tie up

9. an anchor in case there is no rock for tying up
10. a good idea of what the weather and the tide hold in store for you

Stow the gear and tell the Captain you are going. Give him / her an idea of your destination. Step into the center of the dinghy, keep low, and sit down quickly. It doesn't usually happen, but if the dinghy overturns, stay with it. Right the boat by standing on the side of the boat that is out of the water (the windward rail). If it is a sailboat, stand on the centerboard. (Uncleat the sheets first.)

If your destination is a dock, look for the spot where other dinghies are tied up. Observing this courtesy keeps the main docking areas free for larger boats. Before reaching the dock, put out fenders and ship the dockside oar. Remove the oars from the oar-locks and stow them while the dinghy is docked. Remember to pull fenders into the dinghy when underway again.

If you head for the beach, be sure to check the tide table to avoid getting stranded. You may be stuck on dry beach until the tide comes back in, if your dinghy is too heavy to carry.

Beaches are the source of a multitude of interesting things to gather and

Shells

investigate. Take along a plastic bag for shells, stones, edible seaweeds and shellfish. Make sure you have the proper license for gathering water-borne food; most areas require a license for just about everything. When collecting shells, be sure to check that they have no live bodies inside. Depleting the beach is not good; stinky shells with decaying creatures stowed back on the boat are bad, too.

Concerned about the suitability of the shellfish for eating?
In_____ State call this hotline number
for information: (_____) _____

Depending on where you are boating, beware of the deadly and invisible shellfish poison, Paralytic Shellfish Poison (PSP), otherwise known as Red Tide. Always be informed of the Red Tide status. Call the Red Tide hotline number before eating shellfish. The water may be blue and clear today, but yesterday might have been a different story.

If the water is a murky red, use extreme caution when gathering shellfish. Several kinds of microscopic, single-celled animals in masses cause this color and one of them could be the source of Paralytic Shellfish Poison. It affects bivalve mollusks (those with two shells, such as clams, scallops, mussels and oysters) and can be retained in some, for example butter clams, for more than a year.

You will notice that salt water beachcombers talk a lot about Red Tide. They sometimes wonder if the sun-bleached old warning signs...

CAUTION: RED TIDE WARNING.
DO NOT HARVEST THE SHELLFISH

...should be heeded, or if the signs remain posted to keep more shellfish on the beaches for the permanent residents. It's best to believe the signs. Red tide is lethal to humans, and eating contaminated shellfish usually causes speedy death. Red Tide is actually an invisible toxin given off by a type of plankton. Shellfish that have eaten the plankton are healthy, but people die from it. Paralytic Shellfish Poison is tasteless and odorless. Boiling will not get rid of PSP! One clam could kill you! If you have symptoms of tingling lips and tongue, followed by numbness in fingers and toes, call for aid immediately.

Out onto the beach for the afternoon where we are swept clean of duties, of the particular, of the practical. We walk up the beach in silence, but in harmony, as the sandpipers ahead of us move like a corps of ballet dancers keeping time to some interior rhythm inaudible to us.
*— **Gift from the Sea**, Anne Morrow Lindbergh*

On the Beach

Find special stones to put in a shallow dish of water and they will continue to be as beautiful as when you found them.

Stones in dish

Find shells with natural holes in them. Using fishing line and interesting pieces of driftwood, string them together to make wind chimes or a mobile.

Mobile

Bring along a few small wooden picture frames and use glue to secure shells, beach grasses, seaweeds and mosses to create unique photo and mirror frames.

Frame with shells

Look for KELP on saltwater beaches. Use the long whip-like stem as a jump rope. Another unique use for Bull kelp is to create KELP DOLLS. Collect sun-dried bulbs and stems at the high tide line. Cut the stem about five to eight inches away from the top of the bulb. Cut several long skinny pieces from the discarded stem. Soak all in water until just pliable, which will take from one to 20 minutes, depending on the dryness of the kelp. Put a few small stones or dried beans in the bulb, then cinch up the bulb using heavy thread and a needle. This will be the doll's "neck," and the stones will rattle a little.

Kelp dolls

Next, cut two slits for the shoulders. Insert a long skinny piece which will be from the tip of the fingers of one hand to the toes on the same side. Repeat on the other side. You might make tiny slashes for the fingers and toes.

Now you can make slashes at the bottom of the tube creating a skirt. Cut tiny pieces of kelp to make eyes nose, ears, and a mouth and glue them on. Glue on more seaweed for the hair, find something interesting for a necklace and give him/her a rock to sit or stand on... or is s/he dancing? As the kelp dries, the pieces curl and animate the limbs and skirt.

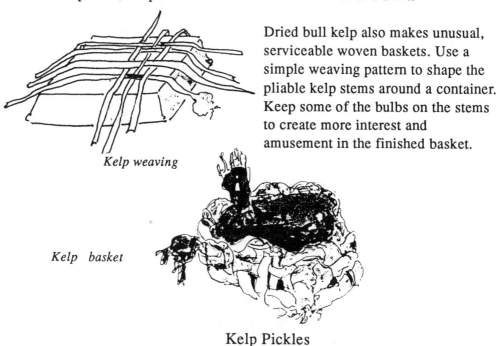

Kelp weaving

Dried bull kelp also makes unusual, serviceable woven baskets. Use a simple weaving pattern to shape the pliable kelp stems around a container. Keep some of the bulbs on the stems to create more interest and amusement in the finished basket.

Kelp basket

Kelp Pickles

If the kelp is fresh, you can make delicious sweet pickles. Use a potato peeler to pare the bulb and stem (discard smaller than 2" across). Cut into 1/2" pieces. Cut enough to measure one quart. Cover the prepared pieces with a salt brine of 1/4 cup salt and 4 cups water. Let soak overnight, rinse well, then use as directed in your favorite watermelon pickle recipe.

Inland

If you are hiking inland, you might watch for some of the many common plants that have food value and will be an interesting addition to galley meals. Often these plants have medicinal uses which are handy to know when you are far away from the corner pharmacy.

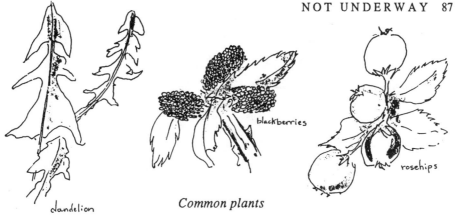

Common plants

A word of caution about satisfying your thirst while foraging: be very careful if you decide to drink from that beautiful, clear stream! A nasty microscopic organism called Giardia Lambia, which causes an intestinal disorder called Giardiasis (otherwise known as "beaver fever"), may be lurking. Contamination is due to animal feces. If you are infected, symptoms include diarrhea, cramps, nausea and loss of appetite. It is curable with medicine and rarely life-threatening, but who needs it? To avoid the risk of Giardiasis, treat all natural water by boiling it for at least one minute, use a water filter or, less effectively, use iodine or chlorine tablets or drops to kill the parasite.

While exploring ashore, be on the look-out for fungus. Some woodsy areas are loaded with interesting forms which, when carved, make great mementos. Experiment with carving a freshly plucked Ganoderma Applanatum, commonly known as "Artist's Conk." It grows abundantly on trees and stumps in North America in a great variety of sizes and shapes. You will see the shelf-like structures extending from trees. Notice how smooth one side is. It must be carved immediately after plucking, for it dries out quickly.

Fungus

Fishing

Guests, especially those who love fishing, usually have a pretty good idea before stepping aboard about opportunities to fish during their particular cruise. It strikes us that there is a huge range of enthusiasm for fishing: there are folks who boat only to fish and are appalled to think of being out on the water without a line and hook in it. At the other end of the scale, there are those who would rather skip what they consider to be the messy, boring part — and fast-forward to a nicely served fillet.

> **When cooking any kind of fish, we have found the Ten Minute Rule successful: measure the fish at its thickest point and cook it for 10 minutes per inch**

No matter where your ardor hits the continuum, you might want to see what all the fuss is about with this pleasant cruising pastime. The ideal set-up is to slip off in the dinghy with a can of beer in your pocket and low expectations of what you will catch.

Spend a couple of hours mulling over life's big questions and contemplating nature. You will most likely end up with something for the galley and a mental tune-up as well.

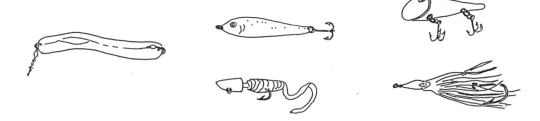

Fishing plugs with hooks

Briefly, there are four ways to fish: casting, jigging, mooching and trolling.

CASTING is useful for catching salmon near the mouths of streams and off beaches. Release, or cast, out the fishing line until the gear hits the water. Pull out a little more line and then reel in slowly, just fast enough to produce action on the line. Repeat. Use shiny spoons, spinners and minnow-like lures.

JIGGING is an excellent way to catch bottomfish off rocky points and near kelp beds. Let the fishing line out until you see slack, then reel it in a few turns. Stay clear of the bottom to avoid snagging your line. Use lead head jigs with plastic worms and various lures. Jigging is also an increasingly popular way to catch salmon with lures such as the "Buzz Bomb" and the "Dart."

MOOCHING is used in tidal rips and off points of land to catch salmon. A mooching type lead sinker that swivels at both ends (two to four ounces in weight) is needed. Attached to the sinker is a mooching leader that typically is six to seven feet long. Herring is used for bait and may be plug cut or fished whole.

To use a plug, first cut off the head at an angle and remove the guts. Secure two hooks in the body so it will spiral as it falls. To use a whole herring, put one hook through the upper lip and another through the back, avoiding the spine, making sure that it will spin as it falls. The depth that you fish will determine what kind of salmon will be on the table. Coho or Silvers are fished in the top 40 feet and Chinooks or Kings are fished near the bottom in depths that range from around 90 to 140 feet or deeper.

TROLLING is perhaps the most popular method to catch salmon and is recommended for novice fishers. Motor very slowly along but fast enough to produce action on the bait or lure. An effective set-up is to use a flasher and fly or squid behind the weight. The depth that you fish (the amount of line let out and the amount of lead used) depends on what kind of salmon you are pursuing.

Some fishing rules

- keep all movements deliberate and controlled (a hook, rod, reel or fish is not a pleasant thing to have tangled in one's hair)

- keep your line clear of the propeller

- watch out for the other fishers

- learn to bait your own line (or invite someone REALLY nice to go with you)

- keep your rod tip up

Knot for tying on hook

- keep your line tight and pointed toward the fish when you have a fish on (a slack line is an opportunity for fish freedom)

- kill your fish immediately and keep it cool

- clean your fish as soon as possible

If you are traveling to a remote area, be sure to buy the appropriate fishing license before leaving. Ask the Captain for information (when, where, how much, what gear) and ask for some local fishing tips at a hardware store.

Hold on to your tackle box, folks! Ever seen or caught one of the magnificent Pacific halibuts? This fish is often so big (females can reach 500 pounds!) that fishermen have to shoot their catch before hauling it aboard. Broken bones (human) and smashed boats are highly likely if a large, angry halibut is thrashing around on board.

Sally's crew was surprised to bring up a 70-pound halibut, but in the excitement neglected to kill it before gaffing and dragging it over the rail. The halibut went berserk, flinging itself about and causing a huge mess on the deck. A lucky flip finally landed him on his back, and an intrepid guest began to rub his belly with the gaff (a metal hook attached to a pole). The halibut was fooled into believing himself rubbing along the bottom of the sea, and quieted long enough to be dispatched. The boat was saved, the crew uninjured, and many wonderful meals were enjoyed. Tickling the tummy...not a bad thing to keep in mind for bottom fish and other sea creatures.

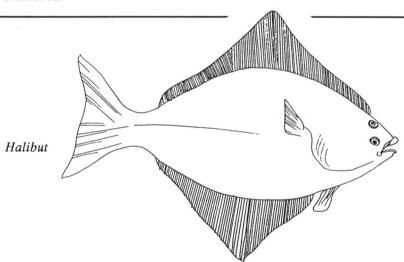

Halibut

Shellfish Gathering: Mollusks and Crustaceans

Continue exploring your area, discovering what is available on the shore and in the inter-tidal areas. A fresh feast from the waters is entirely possible, but be sensitive to local restrictions. Most places require licenses, have limits according to season, oblige closures due to propagation or contamination and also may be subject to changes based on Native American tribal negotiations. Avoid trespassing on private tideland.

Clams, oysters, mussels, scallops, squid and octopus are all mollusks; lobster, shrimp, crabs and crayfish are crustaceans. Each has distinctive flavors ranging from sweet to briny, depending on the location and time of harvesting.

Bivalve (two shelled) mollusks can be affected by contamination from sewage, agricultural run-off and Red Tide (Paralytic Shellfish Poison), so take a good look around your harvesting site for possible trouble.

Sensible Conservation Rules

Replace rocks, fill in holes, take crustaceans sparingly, and know the regional fish and wildlife regulations.

Avoid removing mussels from pilings and taking anything else from impure waters. Oysters should be cleaned on the same beach you found them to prevent spreading the destructive Japanese Oyster Drill. This is a non-migratory predator that you can stop by leaving shells on the same beach. Leaving the shells also allows the beds to re-seed.

Shrimp

Crustaceans require some equipment and attention to details on the way from sea to table. Pots and traps must be attached with non-floating line to a floating buoy (with the owner's name clearly marked on it). The length of the line depends on what you are trapping: crab pots are usually placed in water from 20 to 150 feet (most crabs, however, are caught in less than 60 feet of water), and shrimp are found deeper, sometimes as far as 300 feet down. Tie all lines securely so that you'll be sure of retrieving the trap and so that the buoy will still be connected.

Wire or tie the bait firmly to the center of the trap. Look for landmarks when you drop the trap, so you'll be able to relocate your booty.

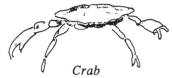

Crab

Good Guests volunteer to "check the pots," an entertainment that can be thrilling or disappointing, but always is great for the biceps. Know the minimum size and maximum quantity limits so you may return the unwanted ones as soon as possible.

Crabs are measured in a straight line across the widest part of the shell, from the outside points; shrimp are measured from the end of the tail to the tip of the rostrum or nose. Female crabs should be returned to protect the stock.

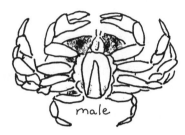

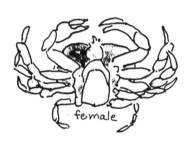

Male & female crabs

Female crabs have a horizontally ridged, wider abdomen compared to the males.

If you must pick up a crab, be careful of the pincers! Grasp it firmly from its rear end or by its rear legs and avoid dropping it near your bare toes!

We always use sea water to cook the crab and shrimp. Extra salt may be added. To cook, drop the shellfish into a deep pot at a rolling boil, cook, then cool quickly in cold water.

Crabs take about 15 to 20 minutes and shrimp 5 to 8 minutes depending on the size. Clean, discarding shells back into the sea, and eat!

Ye gentlemen of England
That live at home at ease,
Ah! little do you think upon
The Dangers of the seas.
— Song, Martin Parker

6
SAFETY

Boating safety is a big factor in determining how much you will enjoy your cruise. Millions of people spend lots of time safely cruising the lakes and seas without ever experiencing an unfortunate incident. Boating courses are offered throughout the United States to ensure that skippers are adequately prepared to handle their boats well. Your Captain and Mate should have enough nautical education and common sense to deal with routine boat handling. If you have any questions, just ask before coming on board.

You, the Good Guest, need to inform yourself about basic safety on the vessel. Some Captains are very bossy about safety measures. Sometimes it's annoying, but listen and learn — there is usually a good reason for the rules. The Bad Captain is inattentive to details which may, in the long run, prove dangerous to all.

- **Know the location of the life jackets, life raft, life ring, fire extinguishers, flares and flashlight.**

- **Ask for instructions in basic safety drills.**

- **Understand what an emergency is and what you should do during one.**

Lifejacket

Locations

Note the location of life jackets, life raft, fire extinguishers, flashlight, and flares on this boat: (Captain will fill in information)

> The life jackets are. . . . .
>
> The life raft is . . . .
>
> The fire extinguishers are   . . . .
>
> The flashlight is   . . . .
>
> The flares are . . . .

The information in this chapter was inspired by infrequent, but scary, news of disasters at sea. We confess to suffering occasional nightmares of worst-case scenarios and feel it's best to talk about how to cope lest anxiety spoil the trip.

Fire extinguisher

Fire extinguisher

For example, suppose you are alone on the boat while it is at anchor. Off in the distance you see a dreadful event, a collision, a capsizing with injuries, an explosion, whatever. Worse yet, what if the Captain and crew suddenly fall to the deck, unconscious. Unlikely, yes, but ... Do you know how to use the VHF radio to call for help?

Non-emergency radio communication

Channel 16, which is monitored by the Coast Guard, is used for distress and safety communications, and calling. Once you have called, or hailed, another vessel and made initial contact, agree to a different channel and switch immediately to that channel and continue your conversation. The Captain is required to listen to Channel 16 while underway. Always return to Channel 16 after ending your conversation. If you are considering using the VHF for a non-emergency call, this procedure is followed.

To make a non-emergency call

- listen and make sure there is no "Mayday" in progress.
- listen and avoid interrupting someone else's communication.
- name the boat you are calling three times, followed by your boat name and call sign (Boat, Boat, Boat, this is Vessel, Vessel, Vessel ABC 123).
- if there is no answer, wait two minutes until repeating.
- after making contact, switch to Channel 68, 69, 71, 72 or 78.
- to end the call, say "This is Vessel ABC123" (your boat name and call sign), "Back to 16" and the word "Out."
- return to Channel 16.

Remember that this is a one-way conversation and when you have the button pressed you cannot hear the other person talking. Say "Over" and release the button to hear the other person.

Emergency radio communications

Mayday, Pan-Pan and Securite are the three distress and safety communications calls on Channel 16. The Mayday distress call is to be used only when life or vessel is in immediate danger and assistance is imperative. Mayday is from the French m'aidez, (help me!), implying in full, Venez m'aider — Come and help me!

The two other distress signals are Pan-Pan and Securite (pronounced SAY-CURE-IT-TAY). The Pan-Pan signal, repeated three times, indicates a degree of jeopardy less urgent than Mayday. Securite also repeated three times, is a message about navigational safety (i.e. a deadhead) or a weather warning. If you hear any distress call, cease all transmission, listen and follow the situation until help has been provided. Transmissions may resume after you hear the all clear.

The following DISTRESS COMMUNICATIONS FORM should be filled out and posted near the VHF transmitter. It is a communications procedure used particularly for a Mayday call. Remember, with any communication, to speak slowly, calmly and clearly!

DISTRESS COMMUNICATIONS FORM
Make sure your radio is turned on to Channel 16.

1. Press the microphone button and say: MAYDAY MAYDAY MAYDAY.

2. Say: This is _____ (repeat your boat name three times). Then say: _____ (your call letters).

3. Say: MAYDAY_____ (and your boat name).

4. Tell where you are. What navigational aids or landmarks are near? Give your latitude and longitude coordinates if possible.

5. State the nature of your distress.

6. State the number of adults and children on board and nature of injuries, if any.

7. Estimate the seaworthiness of your boat.

8. Describe your boat: _____(type) _____ (length)

_____ (color of hull) _____(color of trim)

_____ (number of masts) _____(draft)_____ (horsepower)

_____ (construction material)

_____(anything else which will help rescuers find you)

9. Say: I will be listening on Channel 16. This is_____ _____ (your boat name and call sign). Over.

10. Release microphone button and listen. Someone should answer. If they do not, repeat the call. If there is still no answer, switch to another channel and begin again.

We all easily recall the internationally recognized distress signal:

SOS (... --- ...)

Its initials most popularly stand for Save our Souls, but other interpretations are Save our Ship, Sink or Swim and Stop other Signals. Actually the true meaning is none of these: the signal arose as a combination of Morse Code dots and dashes (dit dit dit for the S; dah dah dah for the O) and remember! SOS replaced the original signal, CQD, in the early years of the 20th century. CQD may have meant Come Quickly Danger/Distress.

Four major disasters

The four major boating emergencies are Fire in the Engine Room, Flooding, Abandon Ship and Man Overboard. It is not probable that any of these disasters will occur. Your Captain and Mate will know procedures to get all aboard safely through these events, but should any, God forbid, happen, it will be helpful for you to know what to expect and how to assist. In all situations the Captain should be clear about what is expected of you. Ask.

Fire in the Engine Room: the Captain shuts off the engines and fuel. Know where the fire extinguishers are and how to use them. Use them at the Captain's signal.

Flooding: the Captain stops, checks the bilge for water and turns on the pumps. Alert the Coast Guard and prepare to abandon ship. Act on the Captain's signal. What causes flooding? Flooding may be caused by damaging contact with a rock (some are uncharted and, with the Captain's permission, should be marked on the chart), a log or a deadhead, for example.

We are slightly paranoid about deadheads, which are fairly common in logging waters. If you have never seen a deadhead, it's probably because you haven't been watching for one. Deadheads are particularly frightening because only an inch or two of one end of the log may be showing above the water. The remainder of the log, water-soaked and almost ready to pull the top part into the depths, holds the log vertically in the water for a time. Deadheads are almost invisible until you are nearly on top of them because they may be washed over by waves and camouflaged until you are quite close. We feel very lucky to have missed deadheads and, in spite of vigilant watching, are sometimes appalled at how close we have come to hitting them.

The Good Guest will help keep a sharp
lookout for deadheads and other debris.
Calmly report sightings to the
helmsperson.

If it's at all possible, stick a small red
flag into the deadhead to warn other
boaters.

Deadhead with flag

Abandon Ship: The Captain calls the
Coast Guard and issues a Mayday. Put on a life jacket. Help make sure
everyone is accounted for. Launch the life raft and fire the flares at the
Captain's signal. Leave your belongings and calmly disembark.

Man Overboard: Immediately yell "Man overboard!" and continue to yell
until the Captain hears you.

Throw anything that floats near the MOB, taking care not to hit the person.
Use fenders, life ring, cushion, life jacket or whatever is nearby to help the
MOB float and also to mark the location.

The more you throw over, the easier it will be to find the MOB and will
give more things for the MOB to hang on to. Station one person to

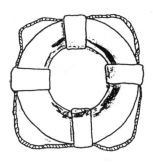

Life ring

continuously watch and point to the MOB.
The helmsperson notes the exact time,
position and compass heading. If your
vessel is a sailboat, drop the sails and start
the engine.

The Captain turns the boat around, slowly
approaches the MOB and comes alongside
to retrieve him/her. When alongside, take
the engine out of gear to avoid fouling the
retrieving line in the prop.

If you are the MOB, scream and yell until you are certain someone has
spotted you in the water. Don't thrash around, but try to assume a fetal
position to retain body heat, keeping your head and shoulders visible so
rescuers will see you.

We continue with more possible dangers, disasters and difficult situations.
Forgive the gloom and doom...

Hypothermia

Should you have the misfortune of being in cold water and waiting to be rescued, your most important task is to delay hypothermia as long as possible by retaining body heat. Swimming will not keep you warm. You will increase your survival time by moving as little as possible and assuming the H.E.L.P, or Heat Escape Lessening Posture, a huddle into the fetal position.

If you have rescued someone with hypothermia, wrap the victim in warm blankets or lie flesh to flesh under covers together to speed up the heating process. Concentrate heat on the core areas (head, neck, chest, groin) to increase warm blood circulation in the vital organs. Avoid warming arms and legs until the core temperature is increased. Add more heat gradually and gently with hot water bottles, warm towels, tub baths. Internally, administer warm steam inhalation.

Do not administer alcohol, which inhibits circulation, and do not allow the victim to smoke for 24 hours.

First aid kits

Most boats carry an adequate first aid kit. But beyond Band-aids and aspirin, guests are responsible for their own supplies and medicines. Guests also must alert the Captain and Mate about food allergies, physical disabilities, and medical conditions which might cause problems while aboard.

Do this well ahead of departure so that adjustments can be made in provisioning the boat.

Situations requiring first aid treatment on board might include: jellyfish stings, bee stings, seasickness, stubbed toes, rope burns, barnacle cuts, sunburn, chapped lips and insect bites.

> In the old days, rum and tar were frequently used for ailments needing antiseptic treatment. Rum was applied to disinfect wounds, kill worms, or thwart colds, and was also thought to restore hair! Tar, applied hot and allowed to cool, would stop bleeding, act as a poultice and, when chewed, was thought to be good for the teeth.

It is worth it to stock up on treatments at your local drug store before boarding.

Seasickness

All things are relative, right? A miserable, although usually not fatal, condition is being seasick. No one chooses to be seasick, but sometimes it happens. The best plan is to fend it off before you are in its clutches. If you face a passage of rough water and suspect you may soon be suffering, find out what prevention and remedies are available on the boat.

We have experimented thoroughly on ourselves and suffering guests and are very sympathetic with those who are afflicted. Here are a few ideas to help get you through difficult waters.

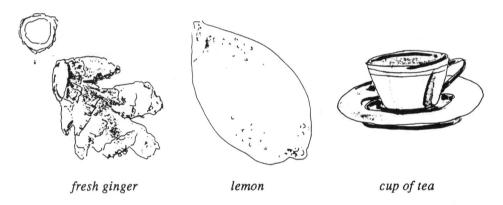

fresh ginger   *lemon*   *cup of tea*

Non-drug suggestions

Sea Bands work very well for some folks. They are small elasticized bracelets that put controlled pressure at a specific point on each wrist. The technique is related to acupressure.

Fresh ginger often wards off seasickness and reduces discomfort from its symptoms. Grate a teaspoon of fresh ginger into a teacup, fill with boiling water, let steep for 10 minutes and drink. Pre-packaged ginger tea is available at health food stores as is green tea, also effective in settling the stomach. (Note: ginger is also said to stimulate digestion, circulation and metabolism, so take along a good-sized piece just in case you need it. For external aches, a hot ginger compress soothes sore spots. Mix two teaspoons of ground ginger with one teaspoon of turmeric and enough water to make a paste, spread it on the area, bandage it and leave it covered overnight.)

Motion Mate, in capsule form, found at health food stores, is fairly reliable for seasick prevention.

If you are qualified to do so, taking your turn at the tiller or wheel is worth a try. As you steer you will be more in sync with the action of the boat, which seems to effectively counteract that topsy-turvy battle going on in your stomach. The Captain may or may not allow your participation at this time, depending on the wildness of the water and your boat handling skills.

Other ideas:

- eat crackers, sunflower seeds or dry toast
- smell a fresh lemon
- get out on deck to watch the horizon and anticipate the waves
- find a place on the boat where the action is calmer (often this is in the stern)
- ask for a task to get your mind off your stomach.
- avoid drinking alcohol.

Drugs to combat seasickness

Gravol works up to six hours and may cause drowsiness. It does not require a prescription.

Bonamine is safe for children and causes less drowsiness. It also does not require a prescription.

Transderm-V, an ear patch, provides relief for up to three days. It is a prescription drug and may cause unpleasant, longer-lasting side-effects. (We are told that women tend to hallucinate with the Patch. A chief mate, while wearing the patch on duty on a commercial vessel, reported sighting trolls marching across the forward deck. Needless to say, she was relieved before her watch was finished!) Many boaters find the Patch brings relief almost instantly and have had no negative side effects. At this writing it is unavailable in the United States.

Coping with other problems

Personal disasters ashore don't seem so bad because medical help is possible with a telephone call. But suppose you are inconveniently far from a dentist while out boating when your tooth breaks off. If you are over 35 years of age, chances are you've a mouth full of old fillings which could crumble off from an unlucky bite.

If a tooth breaks away while you are underway, don't despair. It's possible to do an emergency patch and repair job to let you finish out your trip. For a temporary fix: mix some ZINC OXIDE powder into a few drops of OIL OF CLOVES (eugenol). Thirty five grams of zinc oxide powder is plenty to have on hand, and oil of cloves can be purchased in small quantities and will keep for a long time.

Start by mixing the powder into the oil on a smooth surface (a plate works well). The mixture should resemble putty; add more oil if it is too stiff. Don't rush the mixing. You have plenty of time. Before applying this, dry the tooth and cavity as completely as possible using bits of tissue and tweezers to press gently into the cavity.

When the tooth is dry, roll a small ball of the mixture between your thumb and index finger. Place this in the cavity or over the broken section. Press in gently, clean up excess matter, and close your jaws to check the bite. Try to keep your mouth open and your tongue away from the repair for about five minutes. You may need to file down a sharp, snaggy corner with a small emery board, but the filling should otherwise be serviceable until you can get to a dentist.

If your crown has fallen off, then clean and dry the tooth stub, fill the cap with the temporary "cement" and place it on the tooth. Press firmly, then bite down on a wad of cotton for about five minutes. Clean the tooth area up carefully. Good luck!

WEATHER:
Keeping an eye on it for safety

If the sun sets clear as a bell
It's going to blow sure as hell.

One of the best things about boating is being outside and enjoying the weather. It's always wonderful when the sun is shining and the air is clear, when the clouds build up interesting patterns and the sea sparkles with whitecaps. But when the weather turns and you are sitting in a rain squall, you have more cause for concern than getting a little wet. Weather is the dominant partner of boating.

The Captain takes weather seriously and pays close attention to what it is doing. One important source of information is the barometer, which measures atmospheric pressure and whose subtle fluctuations are to be read with respect. High barometric pressure generally means fine calm weather;

low pressure usually produces bad weather. If the barometer is falling, a low front is headed your way. If it drops significantly, say half an inch, get ready to batten down the hatches. You will be in for a bad session soon.

When the glass falls low,
Prepare for a blow;
When it rises high,
Let your kites fly.

Accurate predictions of fog, storm, wind and calm are crucial to the safety of all aboard. Fortunately, weather channels with up-to-date marine weather forecasts are broadcast on VHF channels continuously in most places. (You may hear announced, for example, "Small craft advisory." This means that winds up to 20 knots are predicted and there will be three-foot waves — hazardous for boats less than 24 feet in length.)

But it may amuse you to keep an eye on the sky and have some knowledge of how the action above will soon affect your cruise. The cloud patterns and formations are often breathtakingly beautiful. We've always felt cloud-gazing is time well spent.

Some cloud terminology:

ALTO = high
STRATUS = layers
NIMBO = rain

Life experience and a wet finger held aloft generally serve well enough for onshore weather predictions, but let's get technical and look at clouds.

The clouds are visible evidence of what is taking place and what will take place shortly. Clouds announce trends in the weather which, if accurately predicted, may give you time to don your rain gear or apply more sunscreen before it's too late.

Four basic types of clouds

CIRRUS has lacey tendrils, showing plumed and feathered "mare's tails". Often the first to appear in the sky, they signify a change in the weather. They are generally high and move in from the northwest. If they are scattered and don't increase, they have little significance. If CIRRUS is in thick patches, rain is close by. Cirrus are high in the sky, up over 25,000 feet.

If (over 20,000 feet) seen as a halo around the sun; can warn of approaching warm front.

Mackerel skies
and mares' tails
Make tall ships
carry small sails.

Cirro stratus

STRATUS clouds have low, gray and uniform bases giving the sky a leaden look. They may indicate fog and there may be a light drizzle. They settle in at about 1,500 feet.

CUMULUS are lumpy, puffy continuously changing shapes, around 4,000 feet. CUMULUS are fair weather clouds. When they swell vertically, heavy showers and gusty winds may be coming.

If clouds are gathering thick and fast
Keep sharp lookout for sail and mast.
But if they slowly onward crawl
Shoot your lines, nets, and trawl.

NIMBUS clouds are low, thick, dark and rain producing, extending over a large area.

Four basic types of clouds:
(top to bottom:
cirrus, stratus, cumulus and nimbus

Was the Walloping Window blind?
No gale that blew dismayed her crew
or troubled the captain's mind.
The man at the wheel was taught to feel
Contempt for the wildest blow,
And it often appeared, when the
weather had cleared,
That he'd been in his bunk below.
— Davey and the Goblin: A Nautical Ballad, Charles Edward Carryl

7
GLOSSARY

ABAFT - behind the widest part of the boat, toward the stern

ABEAM - at a right angle to the boat's center line

AFT - toward the back of the boat

AMIDSHIPS - in the center of the boat

BEACON - a fixed aid to navigation

BEARING - the direction of an object measured relative to the boat's centerline

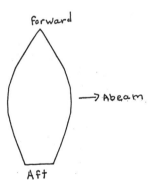

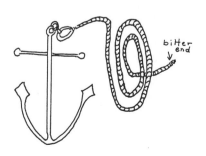

BITTER END - the inboard end of the anchor rode, the extreme end of any line. (This term has always brought to mind a bad taste and puckered face. Historically, the two posts on ships which held the anchor rode or docking lines were called bitts and the turn around the bitt was called the bitter. The end tied at the bitts was called the bitter end.)

BOW - the front end of the boat

BRIDGE - the main control station
of the boat

BUOY - a floating aid to navigation

BULKHEAD - a partition/wall

BURGEE - flag showing owner's
identity to a yacht club or other
organization

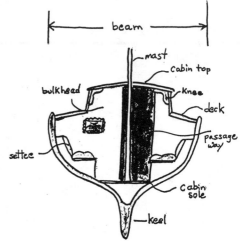

CAN - a cylindrical buoy, usually
green, only identified with odd numbers

CELESTIAL NAVIGATION - use of the stars, sun and moon to determine
position

CHART - a nautical map

CHOCK - a U or an O shaped fitting usually mounted on deck, used to
restrain a line from rubbing on the deck edge

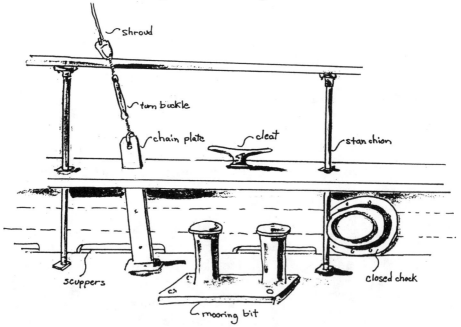

Fittings on a big boat

CLEAT - a fitting to which lines are temporarily attached

COCKPIT - an open space, usually in the stern

COLREGS - the International Regulations for Preventing Collisions at Sea

COMING ABOUT - changing tacks by turning into the wind

COMPANIONWAY - a hatch or entrance from deck to cabin

COMPASS ROSE - a graduated circle carrying the points of the compass and printed on a chart

COURTESY FLAG - another country's flag, flown only when visiting that country

CURRENT - horizontal movement of water

DEADLIGHT - a non-opening port

DEAD RECKONING - the calculation of the boat's position by course and speed

DECK - outside horizontal walking surface

DEPTH SOUNDER - measures the distance between the lowest point of the boat and the sea floor in feet, fathoms or meters

DEVIATION - the effect of iron objects or electrical instruments on the compass reading

DINGHY - a small boat used as a tender

DRAFT - the distance between the waterline and the lowest point of the vessel

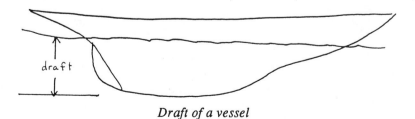

Draft of a vessel

EBB - tidal water flowing out toward the sea

ENSIGN - the national flag of the vessel

FATHOM - one fathom = six feet

FENDER - a cushioning device hung between the boat and another object

FIDDLE RAIL - a device to keep dishes and other objects from sliding off surfaces

Fiddle rail

FIGUREHEAD - a carved figure mounted on the bow. They were considered to be good luck talismans to protect the boat and offer extra eyes to help find the way across the sea. No one knows when they were

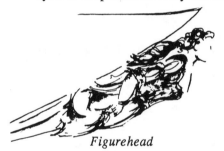

Figurehead

first used, but there is evidence dating to the second century, B.C., on Egyptian ships. In the 18th and 19th centuries, before steamships replaced wooden sailing vessels, figureheads of prominent historic and political leaders, of women, mythological creatures, and dolphins were most popular.

FLOOD - incoming tidal water from the sea

FLYING BRIDGE or FLYBRIDGE - an elevated steering position exposed to the weather

FORWARD - toward the bow

FREEBOARD - the vertical distance between the waterline and the deck edge

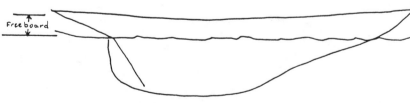

Freeboard

FURL - roll up and secure sails on the yard or boom

GAFF - a spar that sometimes holds the top of a sail

GALLEY - the kitchen

GASKET - ropes or bands of canvas used to make the sails fast to a boom or mast while furling

GEAR - equipment

GIMBALS - pivoted rings which hold objects (a compass or stove for example) and can tip in any direction to keep the object level

Gimballed table

GIVE-WAY VESSEL - the boat that does not have the right of way in a crossing or overtaking situation

GPS (GLOBAL POSITIONING SYSTEM) - a worldwide radio navigation system which uses orbiting satellites

HALYARD - a line used to raise a spar or sail

HATCH - an opening in the deck to give access up or down

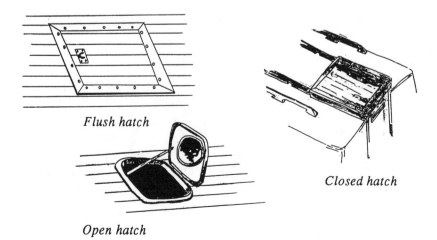

Flush hatch

Closed hatch

Open hatch

HEAD - the toilet (the fixture only or the entire compartment)

HEEL - the boat leaning to one side in
response to the wind and/or waves

HELM - the tiller or wheel

HOLD - storage space below decks

HOUSE FLAG - the owner's private signal
flag, often swallow-tailed in shape, flown
from the mast or bow staff

HULL - the body of a boat

JIB - a triangular sail set forward of the
foremast

Boat heeling

JIBE - to change tacks when sailing downward, by bringing the wind over
the stern

KEEL - the lowest part of the hull, running fore and aft

KEEL HAUL - to haul a person under the hull of a ship as punishment or
torture

KNOT - a unit of speed meaning nautical miles per hour; you never say
"knots per hour." A knot is 1.15 miles per hour; 7 knots roughly equals 8
m.p.h.

LARGE SCALE - a small area shown on the chart with more detail

LATITUDE - the distance north or south of the equator

LAZARETTE - storage space below decks in the stern of the boat

LEAGUE - a distance equal to three nautical miles

LEE BOARD - a board at the side of the bunk to keep you from falling out
during heavy weather.

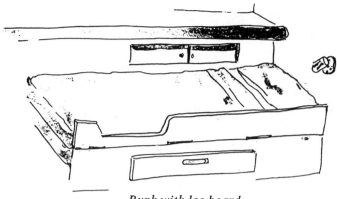

Bunk with lee board

LEEWARD - away from the direction of the wind; the sheltered side

LIST - the boat leans to one side because of uneven loading

LOCKERS - cupboards and closets

LOG BOOK - technical diary of the cruise

LONGITUDE - distance east or west of the prime meridian

LUBBER'S LINE - a fixed line on a compass by which the course is read and the boat steered

MAST - a vertical spar, the main support of the sailing rigging

MAYDAY - the urgent first-priority distress call

METER - a unit of measurement equaling 39.37 inches

MIDSHIPS - the broadest part of the boat

NAUTICAL MILE - 6080.26 feet = 1.1516 statute mile. Distances are measured in nautical miles on salt water. The statute mile is used on shore, in fresh water bodies and along the Intracoastal Waterways.

NUN - a tapering cylindrical buoy, red with even numbers

OVERHEAD - the ceiling of the cabin

PAINTER - tie-up line for the dinghy

PAN-PAN - the second priority urgent call, after Mayday, concerning the safety of the boat, a person on it or in sight of the boat

P.F.D. - Personal Floatation Device; a life preserver

PILOT HOUSE - separate room for steering and navigating

PORT - the left side of the boat

PORTHOLE - windows in the sides of the boat; PORTLIGHTS glass of the windows

PRIVILEGED VESSEL - the boat with the right of way

RADAR - an electronic system using super high-frequency radio waves

RODE - the anchor line or cable

RUDDER - for steering the boat, attached at the stern, controlled by the tiller or wheel

SALON or SALOON - the main living area for common use among passengers

SCUPPER - the drain openings on the deck edge and in the cockpit to allow water to run overboard

SECURITE - the third priority safety messages, after Mayday and Pan-Pan, concerning navigation or weather

SHEET - a line that is used to control a sail

SHIP - a very big boat, never used to refer to a small one. You can put a boat on a ship, but not vice versa.

SHROUDS - fixed rigging that supports the mast at its sides

SLACK WATER - between flood and ebb when there is little or no movement of water

SMALL SCALE - a large area shown with less detail

SOLE - the cabin or cockpit floor

SOS - the international distress signal

SPRING LINE - a dock line leading forward or aft to prevent the boat from moving ahead or astern

Boat with spring lines

STANCHION - a vertical post on the deck

STARBOARD - the right side of the boat

STATEROOM - a private room for sleeping

STERN - the rear of the boat

STOPS - strips of cloth or ropes used to secure a sail to the boom

STOW - put things away

TACK - to change course by turning the bow across the wind

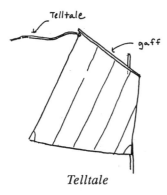

Telltale

TELLTALES - strips of cloth tied high up on the shrouds; they flutter and show you apparent wind direction

TENDER - the small boat used to ferry you to a larger one

TIDE - the vertical rise and fall of sea water

TILLER - lever attached to the rudder, used to control the rudder and steer the boat

Boat's transom

TRANSOM - the transverse part of the stern

UNDERWAY - the movement of a boat, under control of the helmsman and without connection to land

WAY - forward motion of the boat; speed

WHEELHOUSE - a separate room with navigation and steering equipment

WINCH - a mechanical device used to haul on a line

WINDWARD - toward the wind; the boat's weather side

VARIATION - the local differences in degrees between true north and magnetic north

VHF (VERY HIGH FREQUENCY) RADIO - used for communications and direction finding

8
GUEST MEMORIES

This is a place for you, as our honored guest, to write your own
account of a trip or a voyage to share with us and with other guests.
Here you can record some memorable events during your cruise and
general reflections about life afloat.

_____

_____

_____

_____

_____

_____

_____

_____

_____

_____

_____

_____

_____

_____

_____

_____

_____

_____

_____

_____

_____

_____

_____

_____

_____

_____

_____

As far as the eye could see, islands, big and little, crowded all round us — each with its wooded slopes rising to a peak covered with wind blown firs; each edged with twisted junipers, scrub-oak and mosses, and each ready to answer immediately to any name we thought the chart might like it to have. To the north-east, the snow-capped mountains of the coast range reached their jagged peaks for the summer sky. And north, south, east and west, among the maze of islands, winding channels lured and beckoned. That was what we had been doing all day — just letting our little boat carry us where she pleased.
— The Curve of Time, *M. Wylie Blanchet*

Molokai lighthouse

_____

_____

_____

_____

_____

_____

_____

_____

_____

_____

_____

_____

_____

_____

_____

_____

_____

_____

_____

_____

_____

_____

_____

The day was ending in a serenity of still and exquisite brilliance. The water shone pacifically; the sky, without a speck, was a benign immensity of unstained light; the very mist on the Essex marshes was like a gauzy and radiant fabric, hung from the wooded rises inland, and draping the low shores in diaphanous folds.
—Heart of Darkness, *Joseph Conrad*

Cape Flattery lighthouse

If you would not be forgotten,
As soon as you are dead and rotten,
Either write things worth reading,
Or do things worth the writing.
— **Poor Richard's Almanac,** *Benjamin Franklin*

_____

_____

_____

_____

_____

_____

_____

_____

_____

_____

_____

_____

_____

_____

_____

_____

_____

_____

_____

_____

"Glorious, stirring sight!" murmured Toad..."The poetry of motion! The real way to travel! The only way to travel! Here today — in next week tomorrow! Villages skipped, towns and cities jumped — always somebody else's horizons! O bliss! O poop poop! O my! O my!"
— **The Wind in the Willows,** *Kenneth Grahame*

_____

_____

_____

_____

_____

_____

_____

_____

_____

_____

_____

_____

_____

_____

_____

_____

_____

_____

_____

_____

_____

_____

_____

_____

_____

_____

Oh, give me the rover's life — the joy, the thrill, the whirl! Let me feel thee again, old sea! Let me leap into thy saddle once more. I am sick of these terra-firma toils and cares; sick of the dust and reek of towns.
*—**White Jacket,** by Herman Melville*

_____

_____

_____

_____

_____

_____

_____

_____

_____

_____

_____

_____

_____

_____

_____

_____

_____

_____

_____

_____

It was a clear and clear and cloudless night, and the wind blew steady and strong,
As gaily over the sparkling deep our good ship bowled along;
With the foaming seas beneath her bow the fiery waves she spread,
And bending low her bosom of snow she buried her lee cathead.
*—**The Yankee Man of War,** ballad, 1700s*

There's greenhorn fellows, some on board
Before ne'er saw salt water;
When come to sea, upon my word,
The case with them does alter.
—The Jolly Sailor's True Description of a Man-of-War, _ballad, 1700s_

_____

_____

_____

_____

_____

_____

_____

_____

_____

_____

_____

_____

_____

_____

_____

_____

_____

_____

_____

_____

_____

_____

_____

_____

As I lay musing in my bed,
Full warm and well at ease,
I thought upon the lodging hard
Poor sailors had at seas.
—The Praise of Sailors, *ballad, 1600s*

Suggested
Reading List

Young Sailor, by Mark A. Bashforth. Sheridan House, 1993.

Folklore and the Sea, by Horance Beck. Mystic Seaport Museum, Inc., 1985.

The Klutz Book of Knots, by John Cassidy. Klutz Press, 1985.

Scuttlebutt...and Other Expressions of Nautical Origin, by Teri Degen. Henry Holt and Co., Inc., 1989.

Learning to Sail: the Annapolis Sailing School Guide for all Ages,
by Di Goodman and Ian Brody. International Marine TAB Books, 1994.

The Oxford Companion to Ships and the Sea, Peter Kemp, editor. Oxford University Press, 1990.

The Yachtsman's Mate's Guide, by Margie Livingston. Ziff-Davis Publishing, 1980.

Chapman Piloting, by Elbert S. Maloney. Hearst Marine Books, 1994.

A Small Boat Guide to the Rules of the Road, by John Mellor. Fernhurst Books, 1990.

The Stars, by H. A. Rey. Houghton Mifflin Co., 1980.

Edible? Incredible, by Virginia Pill and Marjorie Furlong, Andover Printing and Graphics, 1972.

Discovering Wild Plants, by Janice Schofield. Alaska Northwest Books, 1989.

The Marlinspike Sailor, by Hervey Garrett Smith. The Rudder Publishing Co., 1952.

American Practical Navigator, Bowditch, U.S. Navy Hydrographic Office, 1958.

Chart No.1, Ninth Edition. Department of Commerce and Department of Defense, 1990.

COLREGS—International Rules of the Road.

Index

Barbara Bradfield and Sara Slater are lifelong boaters who have enjoyed many great guests on their boats. They both live on Puget Sound in the Pacific Northwest and their shared interests in boats, books and art inspired this project.